T0234212

iRODS Primer

Integrated Rule-Oriented Data System

Synthesis Lectures on Information Concepts, Retrieval, and Services

iRODS Primer: Integrated Rule-Oriented Data System
Arcot Rajasekar, Michael Wan, Reagan Moore, Wayne Schroeder, Sheau-Yen Chen, Lucas Gilbert, Chien-Yi Hou, Christopher A. Lee, Richard Marciano, Paul Tooby, Antoine de Torcy, and Bing Zhu

Online Multiplayer Games
William Sims Bainbridge

Collaborative Web Search: Who, What, Where, When, and Why
Meredith Ringel Morris and Jaime Teevan

Multimedia Information Retrieval
Stefan Rüger

Information Architecture: The Design and Integration of Information Spaces
Wei Ding and Xia Lin

Hypermedia Genes: An Evolutionary Perspective on Concepts, Models, and Architectures
Nuno Guimarães and Luis Carriço

Reading and Writing the Electronic Book
Cathy Marshall

Understanding User – Web Interactions via Web Analytics
Bernard J. (Jim) Jansen

XML Retrieval
Mounia Lalmas

Faceted Search
Daniel Tunkelang

Introduction to Webometrics: Quantitative Web Research for the Social Sciences
Michael Thelwall

Automated Metadata in Multimedia Information Systems: Creation, Refinement, Use in Surrogates, and Evaluation
Michael G. Christel

Exploratory Search: Beyond the Query-Response Paradigm
Ryen W. White and Resa A. Roth

New Concepts in Digital Reference
R. David Lankes

iRODS Primer: Integrated Rule-Oriented Data System
Arcot Rajasekar, Michael Wan, Reagan Moore, Wayne Schroeder, Sheau-Yen Chen, Lucas Gilbert, Chien-Yi Hou, Christopher A. Lee, Richard Marciano, Paul Tooby, Antoine de Torcy, and Bing Zhu

ISBN: 978-3-031-01143-6 paperback

ISBN: 978-3-031-02271-5 ebook

DOI: 10.1007/978-3-031-02271-5

A Publication in the Springer series

SYNTHESIS LECTURES ON INFORMATION CONCEPTS, RETRIEVAL, AND SERVICES

Lecture #12

Series Editor: Gary Marchionini, University of North Carolina, Chapel Hill

Series ISSN

ISSN 1947-945X print

ISSN 1947-9468 electronic

iRODS Primer

Integrated Rule-Oriented Data System

Arcot Rajasekar
Reagan Moore
Chien-Yi Hou
Christopher A. Lee
Richard Marciano
Antoine de Torcy
Data Intensive Cyber Environments Center and School of Information and Library Science, University of North Carolina at Chapel Hill

Michael Wan
Wayne Schroeder
Sheau-Yen Chen
Lucas Gilbert
Paul Tooby
Bing Zhu
Data Intensive Cyber Environments Center and Institute for Neural Computation, University of California, San Diego

SYNTHESIS LECTURES ON INFORMATION CONCEPTS, RETRIEVAL, AND SERVICES #12

ABSTRACT

Policy-based data management enables the creation of community-specific collections. Every collection is created for a purpose. The purpose defines the set of properties that will be associated with the collection. The properties are enforced by management policies that control the execution of procedures that are applied whenever data are ingested or accessed. The procedures generate state information that defines the outcome of enforcing the management policy. The state information can be queried to validate assessment criteria and verify that the required collection properties have been conserved. The integrated Rule-Oriented Data System implements the data management framework required to support policy-based data management. Policies are turned into computer actionable Rules. Procedures are composed from a Micro-service-oriented architecture. The result is a highly extensible and tunable system that can enforce management policies, automate administrative tasks, and periodically validate assessment criteria.

KEYWORDS

data life cycle, data grid, digital library, preservation environment, policy-based data management, rule engine, iRODS, metadata catalog, assessment criteria, policies, micro-services

Acknowledgments

This research was supported by:

- NSF ITR 0427196, Constraint-Based Knowledge Systems for Grids, Digital Libraries, and Persistent Archives (2004–2007)
- NARA supplement to NSF SCI 0438741, Cyberinfrastructure; From Vision to Reality—Developing Scalable Data Management Infrastructure in a Data Grid-Enabled Digital Library System (2005–2006)
- NARA supplement to NSF SCI 0438741, Cyberinfrastructure; From Vision to Reality—Research Prototype Persistent Archive Extension (2006–2007)
- NSF SDCI 0721400, SDCI Data Improvement: Data Grids for Community Driven Applications (2007–2010)
- NSF/NARA OCI-0848296, NARA Transcontinental Persistent Archive Prototype (2008–2012)

The views and conclusions contained in this document are those of the authors and should not be interpreted as representing the official policies, either expressed or implied, of the National Archives and Records Administration, the National Science Foundation, or the U.S. Government.

Contents

CHAPTER 1

Introduction

Recent decades have seen a rapid rise in collaborative activities in scientific research, and more broadly across many sectors of society. Driven by new information technologies such as the Web as well as the increasing complexity and interdisciplinary nature of today's research problems, from climate change to the world's increasingly integrated economies, the need for technologies, sometimes called "cyberinfrastructure," that enable researchers to collaborate effectively continues to grow rapidly. The Integrated Rule-Oriented Data System (iRODS) is a state-of-the-art software that supports collaborative research, and, more broadly, management, sharing, publication, and long-term preservation of data that are distributed.

A tool for collaboration, iRODS is itself the product of a fruitful collaboration spanning more than a decade among high performance computing (HPC), preservation, and library communities, whose real-world needs have driven and shaped iRODS development. The computational science and HPC communities are inherently interdisciplinary, generating and using very large data collections distributed across multiple sites and groups. The massive size of these data collections has encouraged development of unique capabilities in iRODS that allow scaling to collections containing petabytes of data and hundreds of millions of files.

The preservation community brings the need for long-term preservation of digital information, a challenging problem that is still an active research area to which iRODS research activities have made significant contributions. Interestingly, there turned out to be significant commonalities in the requirements for preserving digital data in time and collaborative sharing of distributed data collections across space, whether geographic, institutional, disciplinary, etc.

The third community that has contributed to iRODS development is the library community, with expertise in descriptive metadata that is essential for management, discovery, repurposing, as well as controlled sharing and long-term preservation of digital collections.

In collaborating with these communities, iRODS research and development has been characterized by close attention to the practical requirements of a wide range of users, resulting in pioneering architecture and solutions to numerous distributed data challenges that now form the iRODS Data System for managing, sharing, publishing, and preserving today's rapidly growing and increasingly complex digital collections.

iRODS is a software middleware, or "cyberinfrastructure," that organizes distributed data into a sharable collection. The iRODS software is used to implement a *data grid* that assembles data into a logical collection. Properties such as integrity (uncorrupted record), authenticity (linking of provenance information to each record), chain of custody (tracking of location and management controls within the preservation environment), and trustworthiness (sustainability of the records) can be imposed on the logical collection. When data sets are distributed across multiple types of storage systems, across multiple administrative domains, across multiple institutions, and across multiple countries, data grid technology is used to enforce uniform management policies on the assembled collection. The specific challenges addressed by the iRODS Data Grid include:

- Management of interactions with storage resources that use different access protocols. The data grid provides mechanisms to map from the actions requested by a client to the protocol required by a specific vendor supplied disk, tape, archive, or object-relational database.
- Support for authentication and authorization across systems that use different identity management systems. The data grid authenticates all access, and authorizes and logs all operations on the files registered into the shared collection.
- Support for uniform management policies across institutions that may have differing access requirements such as different institutional research board approval processes. The policies controlling use, distribution, replication, retention, disposition, authenticity, integrity, and trustworthiness are enforced by the data grid.
- Support for wide-area-network access. To maintain interactive response, network transport is optimized for moving massive files [through parallel input/output (I/O) streams], for moving small files (through encapsulation of the file in the initial data transfer request), for moving large numbers of small files (aggregation into tar files), and for minimizing the amount of data sent over the network (execution of remote procedures such as data subsetting on each storage resource).

In response to these challenges, iRODS is an ongoing research and software development effort to provide software infrastructure solutions that enable collaborative research. The software systems are implemented as middleware that interacts with remote storage systems on behalf of the users. The goal of the iRODS team is to develop generic software that can be used to implement all distributed data management applications, through changing the management policies and procedures. This has been realized by creating a highly extensible software infrastructure that can be modified without requiring the modification of the core software or development of new software code. This publication describes the data grid technology in Chapter 2, the iRODS architecture in Chapter 3, the Rule-Oriented Programming model in Chapter 4, the iRODS Rule system in Chapter 5, the iRODS Micro-services in Chapter 6, examples of iRODS rules in Chapter 7, and extensions to iRODS in Chapter 8. Appendix A lists the iRODS i-Commands that can be executed interactively, Appendix B lists the rulegen grammar, and Appendix C lists exercises that can be used to test knowledge of the iRODS policy-based data management system.

Documentation for iRODS is continually being updated by the growing iRODS open source community on the iRODS wiki at http://www.irods.org, covering topics such as installation, how to use iRODS, administration, and development information. The wiki also contains iRODS-related publications for further reading.

• • • •

CHAPTER 2

Integrated Rule-Oriented Data System

iRODS is software middleware that manages a highly controlled collection of distributed digital objects, while enforcing user-defined Management Policies across multiple storage locations. The iRODS system is generic software infrastructure that can be tuned to implement any desired data management application, ranging from a Data Grid for sharing data across collaborations, to a digital library for publishing data, to a preservation environment for long-term data retention, to a data processing pipeline, to a system for federating real-time sensor data streams.

The iRODS technology, which is developed by the Data Intensive Cyber Environments (DICE) group, is distributed between the University of North Carolina at Chapel Hill (UNC) and the University of California, San Diego (UCSD). The DICE Center has been established at UNC to coordinate development, application, and use of the iRODS Data Grid in cyberinfrastructure. The team at UCSD is associated with the Institute for Neural Computation.

The ideas for the iRODS project have existed for a number of years, and became more concrete through the National Science Foundation-funded project, Constraint-Based Knowledge Systems for Grids, Digital Libraries, and Persistent Archives, which began in the fall of 2004. The development of iRODS was driven by the lessons learned in nearly 10 years of deployment and production use of the DICE Storage Resource Broker (SRB) Data Grid technology and through applications of theories and concepts from a wide range of well-known paradigms from computer science fields such as active databases, program verification, transactional systems, logic programming, business rule systems, constraint-management systems, workflows, and service-oriented architecture. The iRODS Data Grid is an adaptable middleware, in which management policies and management procedures can be dynamically changed without having to rewrite software code.

The iRODS Data Grid expresses management policies as computer actionable Rules, and management procedures as sets of remotely executable Micro-services. The Rules control the execution of the Micro-services. The state information generated by the Micro-services is stored in a metadata catalog (iCAT). The iRODS Data Grid manages input and output information from the

Micro-services (81 Session Variable Attributes and 109 Persistent State Information Attributes), manages composition of 185 Micro-services into Actions that implement the desired management procedures, and enforces 69 active Rules while managing a Distributed Collection. An additional set of eight alternate Rules is provided as examples of the tuning of Management Policies to specific institutional requirements. The Rules and Micro-services are targeted toward data management functions needed for a wide variety of data management applications. The open source iRODS Data Grid is highly extensible, supporting dynamic updates to the Rule Base, the incorporation of new Micro-services, and the addition of new Persistent State Information. With the knowledge provided by this document, a reader will be able to add new Rules, create new Micro-services, and build a data management environment that enforces their institutional Management Policies and procedures.

2.1 DATA GRID OVERVIEW

The iRODS technology builds upon the lessons learned from the first generation of data grid technology developed by the DICE group, the SRB. The same basic concepts needed for distributed data management and organization of distributed data into sharable collections that were implemented in the SRB have also been implemented in iRODS.

The DICE SRB Data Grid is a software infrastructure for sharing data and metadata distributed across heterogeneous resources using uniform Application Programming Interfaces (APIs) and Graphical User Interfaces. To provide this functionality, the SRB abstracts key concepts in data management: data object names, and sets of data objects, resources, users, and groups, and provides uniform methods for interacting with the concepts. The SRB hides the underlying physical infrastructure from users by providing global, logical mappings from the digital entities registered into the shared collection to their physical storage locations. Hence, the peculiarities of storage systems and their access methods, the geographic or administrative location of data, and user authentication and authorization across systems, are all hidden from the users. A user can access files from an online file system, near-line tapes, relational databases, sensor data streams, and the Web without having to worry about where they are located, what protocol to use to connect and access the system, and without establishing a separate account or password/certificate to each of the underlying computer systems to gain access. These Virtualization mechanisms are implemented in the SRB system by maintaining mappings and profile metadata in a permanent database system called the MCAT Metadata Catalog and by providing integrated data and metadata management, which links the multiple subsystems in a seamless manner.

A key concept is the use of *Logical Name Spaces* to provide uniform names to entities located in different administrative domains and possibly stored on different types of storage resources.

When we use the term Logical Name Space, we mean a set of names that are used by the Data Grid to describe entities. Logical Name Spaces are used to describe the users (user Logical Name Space), the files (file Logical Name Space), and storage resources (resource Logical Name Space). An implication is that the Data Grid must maintain a mapping from the logical names to the names understood by each of the remote storage locations. All operations within the iRODS Data Grid are based on the iRODS Logical Name Spaces. The iRODS system internally performs the mapping to the physical names, and issues operations on behalf of the user at the remote storage location. Figure 2.1 shows this mapping from the names used by a storage repository to the logical names managed by iRODS.

Note that the original SRB Data Grid defined three Logical Name Spaces:

1. *Logical names for users.* Each person is known to the Data Grid by a unique name. Each access to the system is authenticated based on either a public key certificate, or Kerberos certificates, or a shared secret.
2. *Logical names for files and collections.* The Data Grid supports the logical organization of the distributed files into a hierarchy that can be browsed. A logical collection can be assembled in which files are logically grouped together even though they reside at different locations.
3. *Logical names for storage resources.* The Data Grid can organize resources into groups, and apply operations on the group of resources. An example is load leveling, in which files are

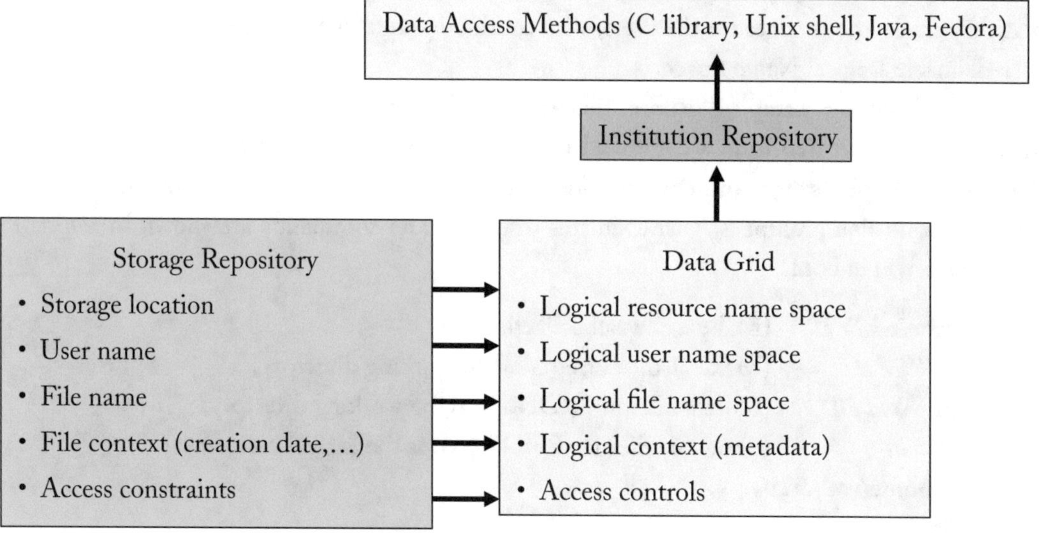

FIGURE 2.1: Mapping from local names to Logical Name Spaces.

distributed uniformly across multiple storage systems. An even more interesting example is the dynamic addition of a new storage resource to a storage group, and the removal of a legacy storage system from the storage group, all transparently to the users of the system.

Both the SRB and iRODS Data Grids implement Logical Name Spaces for users, files, and storage resources. The best example to start with is the logical names for files and directories in iRODS: the Data Object and Collection names. Each individual file stored in iRODS has both a logical and physical path and name. The logical names are the collection and dataObject names as they appear in iRODS. These are the names that users can define and see when accessing the iRODS Data Grid.

The iRODS system keeps track of the mapping of these logical names to the physical files (via storage of the mapping in the iCAT Metadata Catalog). Within a single collection, the individual data objects might exist physically on separate file systems and even on separate host computers. The iRODS system automatically updates the mappings whenever operations are performed on the files, and enables users to access the files (if they have the appropriate authorization) regardless of where the files are located.

This is a form of "infrastructure independence," which is essential for managing distributed data. The user or administrator can move the files from one storage file system (Resource) to another, while the logical name the users see remains the same. An old storage system can be replaced by a new one with the physical files migrated to the new storage system. The iRODS system automatically tracks the changes for the users, who continue to reference the files by the persistent and user-definable Logical Name Space.

The following example illustrates this with the iRODS i-Commands (Unix-style shell commands that are executed from a command line prompt). The full list of i-Commands is given in Appendix A. Explanatory comments are added after each shell command as a string in parentheses. The command line prompt is "zuri%" in this example. The commands are shown in *italics*. The output is shown in **bold**.

zuri% *imkdir t1* (Make a new subcollection t1)
zuri% *icd t1* (Make t1 the current default working directory)
zuri% *iput file1* (Store a file into iRODS into the working directory)
zuri% *ils* (Show the files in iRODS, that is the logical file names)
/zz/home/rods/t1:
file1
zuri% *ils -l* (Show more detail, including the logical resource name)

/zz/home/rods/t1:
rods 0 demoResc 18351 2008-11-17.12:22 & file1
zuri% *ils -L* (Show more detail, including the physical path where the file was stored)
/zz/home/rods/t1:
rods 0 demoResc 18351 2008-11-17.12:22 & file1
/scratch/slocal/rods/iRODS/Vault/home/rods/t1/file1

The first item on the *ils* output line is the name of the owner of the file (in this case, "rods"). The second item is the replication number, which we further explain below. The third item is the Logical Resource Name. The fourth item is the size of the file in bytes. The fifth item is the date. The sixth item ("&") indicates the file is up-to-date. If a replica is modified, the "&" flag is removed from the out-of-date copies.

In the example above, the iRODS logical name for the file was "file1" and the file was stored in the logical collection "/zz/home/rods/t1". The original physical file name was also "file1". The logical resource name was "demoResc". When iRODS stored a copy of the file onto the storage resource "demoResc", the copy was made at the location:

"/scratch/slocal/rods/iRODS/Vault/home/rods/t1/file1"

Any storage location at which an iRODS Server has been installed can be used for the repository through the "-R" command line option. Even though the example below stores "file2" on storage resource "demoRescQe2", both "file1" and "file2" are logically organized into the same logical collection "/zz/home/rods/t1".

zuri% *iput -R demoRescQe2 file2* (Store a file on the "demoRescQe2" vault/host)
zuri% *ils*
/zz/home/rods/t1:
file1
file2
zuri% *ils -l*
/zz/home/rods/t1:
rods 0 demoResc 18351 2008-11-17.12:22 & file1
rods 0 demoRescQe2 64316 2008-11-17.12:29 & file2
zuri% *ils -L*
/zz/home/rods/t1:
rods 0 demoResc 18351 2008-11-17.12:22 & file1
/scratch/slocal/rods/iRODS/Vault/home/rods/t1/file1

```
rods      0 demoRescQe2      64316 2008-11-17.12:29 & file2
    /scratch/s1/schroede/qe2/iRODS/Vault/home/rods/t1/file2
```

Other operations can be performed on files:

- **Registration** is the creation of iRODS metadata that point to the file without making a copy of the file. The *ireg* command is used instead of *iput* to register a file. In the example below, "file3a" is added to the logical collection. Note that its physical location remains the original file system ("/users/u4/schroede/test/file3") and a copy was not made into the iRODS Data Grid.

```
zuri% ireg /users/u4/schroede/test/file3 /zz/home/rods/t1/file3a
zuri% ils
/zz/home/rods/t1:
  file1
  file2
  file3a
zuri% ils -l
/zz/home/rods/t1:
  rods      0 demoResc         18351 2008-11-17.12:22 & file1
  rods      0 demoRescQe2      64316 2008-11-17.12:29 & file2
  rods      0 demoResc         10627 2008-11-17.12:31 & file3a
zuri% ils -L
/zz/home/rods/t1:
  rods      0 demoResc         18351 2008-11-17.12:22 & file1
      /scratch/slocal/rods/iRODS/Vault/home/rods/t1/file1
  rods      0 demoRescQe2      64316 2008-11-17.12:29 & file2
      /scratch/s1/schroede/qe2/iRODS/Vault/home/rods/t1/file2
  rods      0 demoResc         10627 2008-11-17.12:31 & file3a
      /users/u4/schroede/test/file3
```

- **Replication** is the creation of multiple copies of a file on different physical resources. Note that the replication is done on a file that is already registered or put into an iRODS logical collection.

```
zuri% irepl -R demoRescQe2 file1
zuri% ils
/zz/home/rods/t1:
```

```
    file1
    file1
    file2
    file3a
zuri% ils -l
/zz/home/rods/t1:
    rods    0 demoResc       18351 2008-11-17.12:22 & file1
    rods    1 demoRescQe2    18351 2008-11-17.12:33 & file1
    rods    0 demoRescQe2    64316 2008-11-17.12:29 & file2
    rods    0 demoResc       10627 2008-11-17.12:31 & file3a
zuri% ils -L
/zz/home/rods/t1:
    rods    0 demoResc       18351 2008-11-17.12:22 & file1
        /scratch/slocal/rods/iRODS/Vault/home/rods/t1/file1
    rods    1 demoRescQe2    18351 2008-11-17.12:33 & file1
        /scratch/s1/schroede/qe2/iRODS/Vault/home/rods/t1/file1
    rods    0 demoRescQe2    64316 2008-11-17.12:29 & file2
        /scratch/s1/schroede/qe2/iRODS/Vault/home/rods/t1/file2
    rods    0 demoResc       10627 2008-11-17.12:31 & file3a
        /users/u4/schroede/test/file3
```

The replica is indicated by listing the file twice, once for the original file that was stored in the iRODS "demoResc" storage vault, and once for the replica that was stored in the "demoRescQe2" storage vault. The replication number (the second item on the output line) is listed after the name of the owner. Note that the creation dates of the replicas may be different.

A second critical point is that the operations that were performed to put, register, and replicate files within the iRODS Data Grid, were executed under the control of the iRODS Rule Engine. Computer actionable Rules are read from a Rule Base "core.irb" and used to select the procedures that will be executed on each interaction with the system. In the examples above, a default Policy was used to specify how the path name for each file was defined when the file was written to an iRODS storage resource (vault). The specific default Rule that was used set the path name under which the file was stored to be the same as the logical path name. This makes it easy to correlate files in storage resources with files in the iRODS logical collection. We explain the syntax of this Rule in Chapter 5.2 on iRODS Rules:

```
acSetVaultPathPolicy||msiSetGraftPathScheme(no,1)|nop
```

When managing large numbers of files, the remote physical storage location may have a limit on the number of files that can be effectively stored in a single directory. When too many files are put into a single physical directory, the file system becomes unresponsive. The iRODS Data Grid provides a procedure (Micro-service) that can be used to impose two levels of directories and create a random name for the physical path name to the file. We can replace the default Rule in the "core.irb" Rule Base for controlling the definition of path names with the following Rule:

acSetVaultPathPolicy||msiSetRandomScheme|nop

Once the core.irb file is changed, all subsequent operations will be controlled by the new set of Rules. In the example below, a file is put into the iRODS Data Grid using the new Rule set. We observe that the physical file path is now ". . . /rods/10/9/file4.1226966101" instead of ". . . /rods/t1/file4"—that is, the new Rule assigns a random number at the end of the physical name and creates and uses two levels of directories ("/10/9/") to keep the number of items in each directory sufficiently low. In some cases, this will provide improved performance and greater capacity.

```
zuri% iput file4
zuri% ils
/zz/home/rods/t1:
 file1
 file1
 file2
 file3a
 file3b
 file4
zuri% ils -l file4
 rods       0 demoResc            27 2008-11-17.15:55 & file4
zuri% ils -L file4
 rods       0 demoResc            27 2008-11-17.15:55 & file4
     /scratch/slocal/rods/iRODS/Vault/rods/10/9/file4.1226966101
```

This simple example illustrates why the iRODS Data Grid is viewed as a significant advance over the SRB Data Grid technology. The policy for defining how physical files will be named is under the control of the Data Grid administrator. The SRB Data Grid was a one-size-fits-all system. The policies used in managing the data at the server level were explicitly implemented within the SRB software. Changes to the policies required having to write new SRB software. Also, if a user wanted to perform complex sets of operations on the files, they had to create a script or program that was run at the client level. If a community wanted to perform a different type of operation (say, change the way the access control for files was implemented), they had to change the SRB code with the hope that it did not introduce unintended side effects on other operations.

Requests for such customizable requirements come from the SRB user community itself. For example, one user wanted a feature in which all files in a particular collection should be disabled from being deleted even by the owner or Data Grid administrator, but other collections should behave as before! This kind of collection-level data management Policy is not easily implemented in the SRB Data Grid without a great deal of work. Also, the required software changes are hardwired, making it difficult to reapply the particular SRB Data Grid instance in another project that has a different data deletion policy.

Another example is based on a request to use additional or alternate checks for access controls on sensitive files. This again required specialized coding to implement the capability in the SRB. A third example occurred when a user wanted to asynchronously replicate (or extract metadata from, or create a lower resolution file from) newly ingested files in a particular collection (or for a specific file type). Implementation of this feature required additional coding and asynchronous scheduling mechanisms not easily done in the SRB.

• • • •

CHAPTER 3

iRODS Architecture

The iRODS system belongs to a class of middleware that we term *adaptive middleware*. The Adaptive Middleware Architecture (AMA) provides a means for adapting the middleware to meet the needs of the end user community without requiring that they make programming changes. One can view the AMA middleware as a glass box in which users can see how the system works and can tweak the controls to meet their demands. Usually, middleware is the equivalent of a black box for which no changes are programmatically possible to adjust the flow of the operations, except predetermined configuration options that may allow one to set the starting conditions of the middleware.

There are multiple ways to implement an AMA. In our approach, we use a particular methodology that we name *Rule-Oriented Programming* (ROP). The ROP concept is discussed in some detail in Chapter 4.

The iRODS architecture provides a means for customizing data management functions in an easy and declarative fashion using the ROP paradigm. This is accomplished by coding the processes that are being performed in the iRODS Data Grid system as Rules (see Chapter 5) that explicitly control the operations that are being performed when an Action is invoked by a particular task. These operations are called Micro-services (see Chapter 6 on Micro-services) in iRODS and are C-functions that are called when executing the Rule body. One can modify the flow of tasks when executing the Rules by interposing new Micro-services (or Rule invocations) in a given Rule or by changing and recompiling the Micro-service code. Moreover, one can add another Rule in the Rule Base for the same task, but with a higher priority so that it is chosen before an existing Rule. This preemptive Rule will be executed before the original Rule. If there is a failure in the execution of any part of this new Rule, then the original Rule is executed.

The major features of the iRODS architecture include the following:

1. Data Grid Architecture based on a client/server model that controls interactions with distributed storage and compute resources.

2. A Metadata Catalog managed in a database system for maintaining the attributes of data, and state information generated by remote operations.
3. A Rule System for enforcing and executing adaptive Rules.

The *iRODS Server* software is installed on each storage system where data will be stored. The remote location of the storage system is normally defined by an Internet Protocol (IP) network addresss. The iRODS Server translates operations into the protocol required by the remote storage system. In addition, a *Rule Engine* is also installed at each storage location. The Rule Engine controls operations performed at that site. Figure 3.1 illustrates the components of the iRODS system, including a Client for accessing the Data Grid, Data Grid Servers installed at each storage system, a Rule Engine installed at each storage location, the iCAT Metadata Catalog that stores the persistent state information, and a Rule Base that holds the Rules.

The iRODS Data Grid uses persistent state information to record all attributes that are needed about a file, including the name of the file, the location of the file, the owner of the file, a file

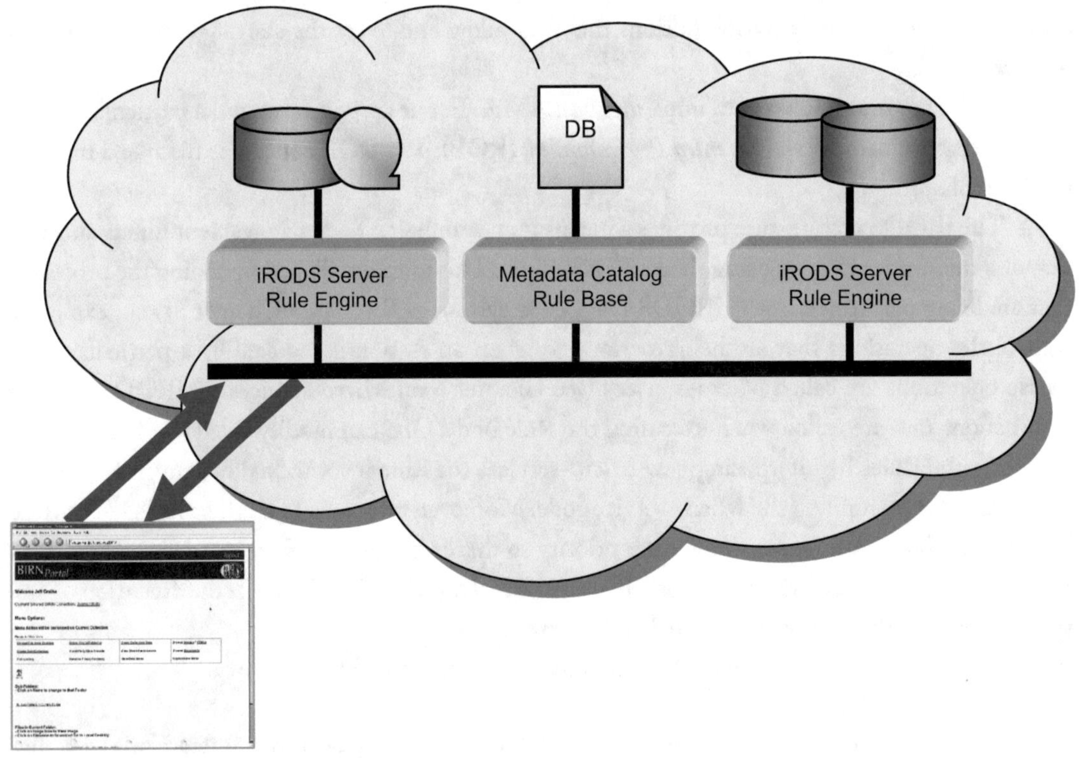

FIGURE 3.1: iRODS peer-to-peer server architecture.

checksum, a data expiration date, and many others. More than 100 attributes are used by iRODS to manage information about each file. The iRODS Data Grid Servers constitute a peer-to-peer server architecture, in which each server can exchange information with any other iRODS Server.

When a user accesses an iRODS Server, information is exchanged between the iRODS Server and the server that hosts the metadata catalog (iCAT-enabled server). The user is authenticated, and the physical location where the user commands will be executed is identified. The users' request is forwarded to the appropriate iRODS Server. The Rule Engine at that location then verifies whether the desired operations can be executed, translates the operations into the protocol required by that type of storage system, and passes the result of the operations back to the iRODS client. Any state information that is generated is registered into the iCAT metadata catalog.

The Rule Base is replicated to each iRODS Server. When the iRODS Server is installed at a particular storage location, an iRODS Rule Base is also installed. Future enhancements to the iRODS system will investigate automated updates to the Rule Base depending on the version that is installed at the coordinating Metadata Catalog site. In the current approach, each site can choose to run a different set of Rules, including Rules that are specific to the type of storage system at the site's location. Since the Rule Engine at the site where the data reside controls the operations performed on the data, it is possible to implement storage resource-specific policies. For example, a storage system that is used as a data cache may impose a policy on all file put operations that automatically replicates the file to a tape archive.

In order to create a highly extensible architecture, the iRODS Data Grid implements multiple levels of *virtualization*. Clients generate task-initiated event–condition–action workflows. As shown in Figure 3.2, the Actions requested by a client are mapped to sets of standard functions, called Micro-services. A single client request may invoke the execution of multiple Micro-services and Rules, which are chained together into a workflow.

In turn, the Micro-services execute standard operations that are performed at the remote storage location. The standard operations are based on the Posix I/O functions listed in Table 3.1. A given Micro-service can invoke multiple Posix I/O calls. Thus, a Micro-service is intended to simplify expression of procedures by providing an intermediate level of functionality that is easier to chain into a desired Action.

The Posix I/O calls are then mapped into the protocol required by the storage system through a driver that is written explicitly for that storage system. The Data Grid Middleware comprises the software that maps from the Actions requested by the *client access interface* to the *storage protocol* required by the storage system.This approach means that new access mechanisms can be added without having to modify the standard operations performed at the storage systems. Also, new types of storage systems can be integrated into the system by writing new drivers without having to modify any of the access clients.

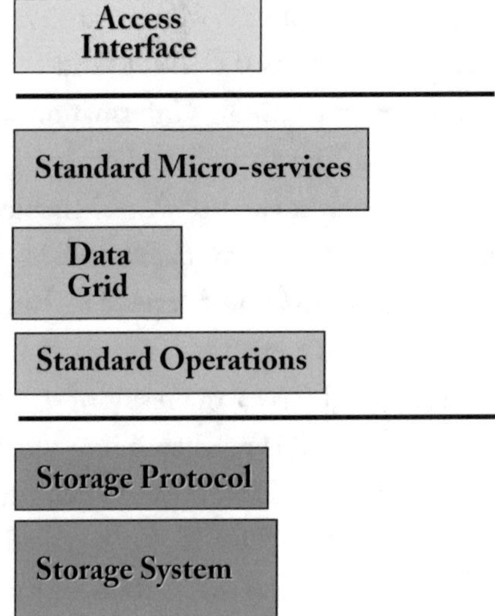

FIGURE 3.2: iRODS architecture.

The list of Posix I/O calls includes the ability to do partial I/O on a file at a storage device. Since not all of the storage systems that may be integrated into the Data Grid have this ability, caching of files on a second storage system may be necessary. This approach was used to support manipulation of files within the mass storage system at the National Center for Atmospheric Research, which only allowed complete file input and retrieval. A copy was made on a disk file system, where partial I/O commands were then executed.

The iRODS Data Grid effectively implements a *distributed operating system*. Consider the operating system on a laptop. It supports computation, scheduling of applications, data movement,

TABLE 3.1: POSIX I/O commands.

Open a file	Open a directory	Seek to a location in a file
Create a file	Make a directory	List information about files
Close a file	Close a directory	Display file status
Unlink a file	Remove a directory	
Read a file	Read a directory	Change access permission
Write a file		Force completion of disk write

and data storage, and maintains internal tables that track the results of all operations. The iRODS Data Grid also supports computation (execution of Micro-services), scheduling of Rules for deferred execution, data movement between servers, and storage of data, and maintains the persistent state information in a database. The difference is that iRODS implements an environment that uses multiple servers located at distributed sites that are under the control of multiple administrative domains.

For the iRODS Data Grid to work effectively, the data that are moved between the distributed servers have to be linearized for transmission over a network. The remote operations generate Structured Information that is passed between Micro-services and the Client. The data Structures are specific to each Micro-service. The requirement that the Structured Information be carefully defined is actually a major advantage, in that it then becomes possible to chain multiple Micro-services together. The structure of the output from one Micro-service can be mapped to the required structure for input into another Micro-service.

The iRODS framework implements multiple mechanisms needed to control the exchange of Structured Information, the execution of the remote Micro-services, and the interactions between the Rule Base, Rule Engine, Metadata Catalog, and network. The iRODS framework is illustrated in Figure 3.3. The components include:

- **Data Transport**—Manages parallel I/O streams for moving very large files (greater than 32 Megabytes in size) over the network. An optimized transport protocol is used that sends the data with the initial transfer request for small files less than 32 Megabytes in size.
- **Metadata Catalog**—Manages interactions with a vendor-specific or open source database to store descriptive metadata and Persistent State Information.
- **Rule Engine**—Manages the computer actionable Rules to control selection of Micro-services.
- **Execution Control**—Manages scheduling of the Micro-services that are selected by the Rule Engine. Micro-services may be executed at multiple storage locations, or deferred for execution, or executed periodically.
- **Execution Engine**—Manages execution of a Micro-service. The Micro-services are written in the "C" language, and are compiled for a specific operating system. The execution engine manages the input of data to the Micro-service, and manages the output of data from the Micro-service.
- **Messaging System**—Manages high-performance message exchange between iRODS Servers. This is required when Structured Information is moved between Micro-services that are executed at different storage locations.
- **Virtualization Framework**—Coordinates interaction between the framework components.

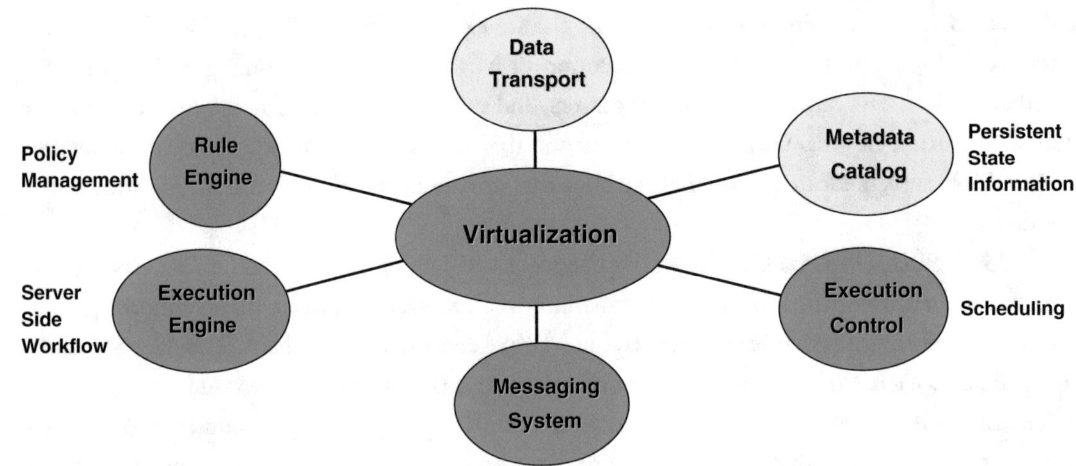

FIGURE 3.3: iRODS distributed operating system.

The mechanisms implemented within the iRODS system are very powerful. They are able to control the execution of workflows at each remote storage location. This linking of multiple remote procedures is called a *server-side workflow* to differentiate it from workflows executed at a compute server under the control of a client (*client-side workflows*). Examples of client-side workflows are grid computing process management systems such as Kepler and Taverna. They typically move data to the computer, process the data, and then move the result to a storage location. The iRODS system effectively moves the computation to the storage location (in the form of a Rule that will be executed), applies the Rule, and stores the result. This implies that a Rule represents a workflow that will be executed to implement a desired Client task.

The types of workflows that should be executed directly on a storage system have low complexity—a small number of operations compared to the number of bytes in the file. If the complexity is sufficiently small, then the amount of time needed to perform the workflow will be less than the time that would have been required to move the file to a compute server. For workflows that have high complexity, it is faster to move the file to a compute server than it is to perform the operations at the remote storage system.

Thus, iRODS is expected to control low-complexity workflows that can be most efficiently executed at each storage system. Examples of low-complexity workflows include the extraction of a data subset from a large file, or the parsing of metadata from a file header.

An implication of the restriction to low-complexity workflows is that the iRODS system should interact with remote computers to execute high-compexity tasks. This capability is currently enabled through support for encapsulation of remote web services as iRODS Micro-services.

Within the iRODS workflow, calls can be issued to remote processing systems that manipulate data that can be moved across the network. The iRODS Rule Base uses a well-defined set of Micro-services that can be written for specific data format manipulation. The Rule Base should encompass a small number of Rules that are highly tuned to the specific data management policies for which the shared collection was created.

3.1 VIRTUALIZATIONS IN iRODS

iRODS provides a new abstraction for data management processes and policies (using the logical Rule paradigm) in much the same manner that the SRB provided new abstractions for data objects, collections, resources, users, and metadata. iRODS characterizes the Management Policies that are needed to enforce *authenticity*, *integrity*, *chain of custody*, *access restrictions*, *data placement*, and *data presentation*, and to automate the application of Policies for services such as administration, authentication, authorization, auditing, and accounting, as well as data management policies for retention, disposition, replication, distribution, pre- and post-processing and metadata extraction, and loading. The Management Policies are mapped onto computer actionable Rules that control the execution of all data management operations. iRODS can be seen as supporting four types of virtualization beyond those supported by a Data Grid such as the SRB.

- **Workflow virtualization.** This is the ability to manage the execution of a workflow that is distributed across multiple compute resources. The management of the workflow execution is done independently of the compute resources where the workflow components are executed. This requires the ability to manage the scheduling of the executing jobs and the tracking of their completion status. iRODS implements the concept of workflows through chaining of Micro-services within nested Rule sets and through using shared logical variables that control the workflow. The Micro-services can share information (output from one Micro-service used as input to the next Micro-service) through structures in memory, or by transmission over a network. To send complex structures to a remote server, the structures are serialized (turned into a linear sequence of bytes) by packing routines, and then turned back into the desired structure by unpacking routines at the remote location.
- **Management policy virtualization.** This is the expression of Management Policies as Rules that can be implemented independently of the choice of remote storage system. The Policies control what happens within the data grid. A user request is interpreted as a set of tasks that need to be executed. Each task initiates a set of event–condition–actions. Before an action is executed, a pre-process management policy is checked for operations that should be performed. A typical operation is checking for permissions needed to execute

the action. Once the action is completed, a post-process management policy is checked for additional operations to perform. An example is creating a thumbnail image on ingestion of a jpeg image.

We characterize Management Policies in terms of *policy attributes* that control desired outcomes. Consider a policy to minimize risk of data loss. A policy attribute is the number of replicas that will be made for each file within the data grid to minimize risk of data loss. The integrity policy attribute is the "number of replicas." For each desired outcome, Rules are defined that control the execution of the standard remote operations. On each Rule application, Persistent State Information is generated that describes the result of the remote operation. Consistency Rules (or assessment criteria) can be implemented that verify that the remote operation outcomes comply with the Policy Attributes. Rule-based data management infrastructure makes it possible to express Management Policies as Rules and define the outcome of the application of each Management Policy in terms of updates to the Persistent State Information. iRODS applies the concept of transactional Rules using datalog-type Event–Condition–Action Rules working with persistent shared metadata. iRODS implements traditional ACID (Atomicity, Consistency, Isolation, Durability) database properties.

- **Service virtualization.** The operations that are performed by Rule-based data management systems can be encapsulated in Micro-services. A Logical Name Space can be constructed for the Micro-services that makes it possible to name, organize, and upgrade Micro-services without having to change the Management Policies. This is one of the key capabilities needed to manage versions of Micro-services, and enable a system to execute correctly while the Micro-services are being upgraded. iRODS Micro-services are constructed on the concepts of well-defined input–output properties, consistency verification, and roll-back properties for error recovery. The iRODS Micro-services provide a compositional framework realized at run-time.
- **Rule virtualization.** This is a Logical Name Space that allows the Rules to be named, organized in sets, and versioned. A Logical Name Space for Rules enables the evolution of the Rules themselves.

3.2 iRODS COMPONENTS

The iRODS system consists of iRODS Servers that are installed at each storage location, a central iRODS Metadata Catalog or iCAT, and Clients. The iRODS Server contains both the driver that issues the local storage resource protocol and the iRODS Rule Engine that controls operations performed at the storage location. The components of the iRODS system are shown in Figure 3.4.

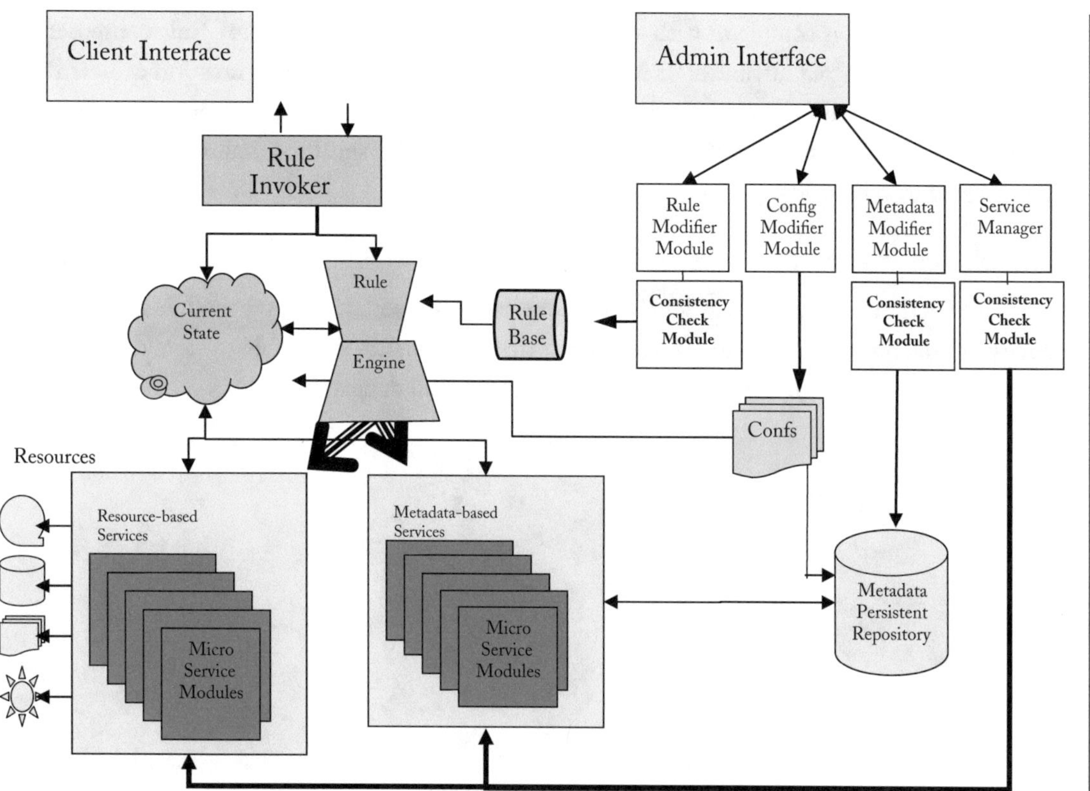

FIGURE 3.4: iRODS architecture components.

The client interface is typically built on either a C library interface to the iRODS Data Grid or a Java I/O class library, or uses Unix-style shell commands. These interfaces send messages over the network to an iRODS Server. The server interacts with the iRODS iCAT Metadata Catalog to validate the user identity, and authorize the requested operation. The location where the operation will be performed is identified, and the operation request is forwarded to the remote storage location. The Rule Engine at the storage location selects the Rules to invoke (Rule Invoker) from the Rule Base, retrieves current state information as needed from the Configuration files and the Metadata Persistent Repository, stores the current state information in a Session memory, and then invokes the Micro-services specified by the Rules.

An important component that is under development is an extended administrator interface. As Rules, Micro-services, Resources, and Metadata are changed, the consistency of the new system must be verified. The architecture design allows for the execution of consistency Modules to verify that the new system is compliant with selected properties of the old system. A Rule composer that checks input and output attributes of Micro-services is needed to simplify creation of new Rules. The Data Grid Administrator manages and designs the Rules used by iRODS, and executes administrative functions through the i-Command “iadmin”. The specific administrative commands can be listed by typing

iadmin –h

Interaction with the storage location is done through a software driver module that translates requests to the protocol of the specific storage device. This makes it possible to store data in a wide variety of types of storage systems, including disks, tape, and databases.

• • • •

CHAPTER 4
Rule-Oriented Programming

ROP is a different (although not new) paradigm from normal programming practice. In ROP, the power of controlling the functionality rests more with the users than with system and application developers. Hence, any change to a particular process or policy can be easily constructed by the user, and then tested and deployed without the aid of system and application developers.

ROP can be viewed as lego-block type programming. The building blocks for the ROP are "Micro-services." Micro-services are small, well-defined procedures/functions that perform a specific task. Micro-services are developed and made available by system programmers and application programmers. Users and administrators can "chain" these Micro-services to implement a larger macro-level functionality that they want to use or provide for others. For example, one of the Micro-services might be to "createCollection", another one might be to "computeChecksum", and a third to "replicateObject".

Larger macro-level functionalities are called Actions. Since one can perform an Action in more than one way, each Action might have one or more chains of Micro-services associated with it. Hence, one can view an Action as the name of a task, and the chains of Micro-services as the procedural counterpart for performing the task. Since there may be more than one chain of Micro-services possible for an Action, iRODS provides two mechanisms for finding the best choice of Micro-service to apply in a given situation. The first mechanism is a "condition" that can be attached to any Micro-service chain, which will be tested for compliance before executing the chain. These conditions, in effect, act as guards that check for permission for execution of the chain. The triplet ⟨action, condition, chain⟩ is called a "Rule" in the ROP system. (There is another concept called "recovery Micro-services chain," which will be introduced later, that will increase the Rule components to a quartet.)

The second mechanism that is used for identifying an applicable Rule is a "priority" associated with a chain. Priority is an integer associated with a Rule that identifies the order in which it will be tested for applicability: the lower the number, the higher the priority. In the current implementation, the priority is associated with the way the Rules are read from Rule files upon initialization.

The earlier the Rule is read and included in the Rule Base, the higher its priority compared to all the Rules for the same Action.

The implementation of iRODS includes another helpful feature. The chain of Micro-services is not limited to only Micro-service procedures and functions, but can also include Actions. Hence, when executing a chain of Micro-services, if an Action needs to be performed the system will invoke the Rule application program for the new Action. Thus, an Action can be built using other Actions. Care should be taken so that there are no infinite cycles in any loop formed by recursive calls to the same Action.

In summary, the first three components of a Rule consist of an action name, a testable condition, and a chained workflow consisting of actions and Micro-services. Each Rule also has a priority associated with it.

The fourth component of a Rule is a set of recovery Micro-services. An important question that arises is, what should be done when a Micro-service fails (returns a failure). A Micro-service failure means that the chain has failed and hence that the instance of the Action has failed. But as mentioned above, there can be more than one way to perform an Action. Therefore, when a failure is encountered, one can try to execute another Rule of a lower priority for that Action. When doing this, a decision must be made about the changes that were made to variables generated by the failing chain of Micro-services. In particular, any side effects (such as a physical file creation on a disk) that might have happened as a result of successful Micro-service execution before the failure must be handled. The same question applies to any changes made to the metadata stored in the iCAT.

The iRODS architecture is designed so that if one Rule for an Action fails, another applicable Rule of lower priority is attempted. If one of these Rules succeeds, then the Action is considered successful. To make sure that the failing chain of Micro-services does not leave any changes and side effects, we provide the following mechanism. For every Micro-service in the chain in a Rule, the Rule designer specifies a "recovery Micro-service or Action" that is listed in the same order as in the chain.

A recovery Micro-service is just like any Micro-service, but with the functionality that it recovers from the task rather than performs a task. A recovery Micro-service should be able to recover from the multiple types of errors that can result from an execution of the corresponding Micro-service. More importantly, a recovery Micro-service should also be able to recover from a successful Micro-service execution! This feature is needed because in the chain of Micro-services, when a downstream Micro-service fails, one needs to recover from all changes and side effects performed, not only those of the specific failing Micro-service but also those of all the successful Micro-services in the chain performed before the failed Micro-service. The recovery mechanism for an Action is of the same type as that of a recovery Micro-service, although one only needs to recover from successful completion of a Rule, when a later Micro-service/Rule fails in the chain. If an Action fails, by definition, any Rule for that Action would have recovered from the effects of the failed Action!

During the recovery process, the recovery Micro-services for all the successful Micro-services will be performed, so that when completed, the effect of the Rule for that Action is completely neutralized. Hence, when an alternate, lower priority Rule is tried for the same Action, it starts with the same initial setting used by the failed Rule. This property of complete recovery from failure is called the "atomicity" property of a Rule. Either a Rule is fully successful with attendant changes and side effects completed, or the state is unchanged from the time of invocation. If all Rules for a particular Action fail, one can see that the system is left in the same state as if the Rule was not executed. One can view this as a "transactional" feature for Actions. The concepts of atomicity and transactions are adopted from relational databases.

In summary, every Rule has an Action name, a testable condition, a chain of Actions and Micro-services, and a corresponding chain of recovery Actions and Micro-services. Each Rule also has an associated priority.

For example, consider a very simple Rule for data ingestion into iRODS, with two Micro-services, "createPhysicalFile" and "registerObject", and no conditions. The Rule creates a copy of the file in an iRODS storage vault and registers the existence of the file into the iCAT Metadata Catalog. The Data Grid administrator can define an alternate Rule of a higher priority, which can also check whether the data type of the file is "DICOM image file" and invoke an additional Micro-service called "extractDICOMMetadata" to populate the iCAT with metadata extracted from the file, after the file has been created on the iRODS Server and registered in the iCAT Metadata Catalog.

We did not implement the idea that an Action or Micro-service should be implicitly tied to a single recovery Action or Micro-service. Although this might make it easier to find a recovery service by this implicit link, we recognized that recovery from an Action or Micro-service can be dependent on where and how it is being invoked. Sometimes, a simpler recovery would do the trick instead of a more complex recovery. For instance, a database rollback might suffice if one knew that the Action started a new iCAT Metadata Catalog database transaction. Otherwise, a longer sequence of recovery delete/insert and update SQL statements is needed to recover from multiple SQL statement activities. So, we give the Rule designer the ability to tie in the appropriate recovery for each Micro-service or Action as part of the Rule instead of having the system or application designer who develops the Micro-service do this.

The Rules for version 2.1 of iRODS are stored in "iRODS Rule Base" files (files with extension ".irb"). These files are located in the server/config/reConfigs directory. One can specify use of more than one irb file that will be read one after the other during initialization. The set of irb files to be used is decided by the iRODS administrator by setting values for the variable reRuleSet in the server/config/server.config file. The administrator can include more than one Rule Base file, by setting the value in a comma-separated manner. The files will be read in the order they are given in the list (left-to-right) and the Rules are prioritized in the order they are read. By default, the Rule Base to be used is set to the core.irb file.

Now that we have seen what comprises a Rule, an Action, and a Micro-service, we will next look at how a Rule is invoked and what type of mechanisms are available to communicate with the Micro-services and Actions. As one can see, Micro-services (by this, we also mean Actions) do not operate in a vacuum. They need input and produce output and communicate with other Micro-services, make changes to the iCAT database, and have side effects such as file creation. Hence, the question arises, what information do the Rules operate on?

To answer this question, we need the concept of a *session*. A session is a single iRODS Server invocation. The session starts when a client connects to the iRODS Server and ends when the Client disconnects. During the session, there are two distinct "state information" spaces that are operated upon by Actions and Micro-services:

- **Persistent State Information** (denoted by the symbol #) is defined by the attributes and schema that are stored in the iCAT catalog.
- **Session State Information** (denoted by the symbol $) is temporary information that is maintained in the memory as a C-structure only during the period when the Actions are being performed.

The Persistent State Information (denoted by #) is the content that is available across sessions and persists in the iCAT Metadata Catalog after the Action has been performed, provided proper commit operations were performed before the end of the session. The Session State Information (denoted by $) does not persist between sessions but is a mechanism for Micro-services to communicate with each other during the session without going to the database # to retrieve every attribute value. One can view the # as a "persistent blackboard" through which sessions communicate with each other (sessions possibly started by different users). Similarly, one can view $ as a "temporary blackboard" that manages within a session some of the state information needed by Actions and Micro-services. Note that $ persists beyond a single Action, and hence when one is performing multiple Actions during a single session, the memory of the earlier Actions (unless destroyed or overwritten) can be utilized by a current Action.

The $ structure is a complex C structure, called the Rule Execution Infrastructure (REI). The REI structure will evolve during the implementation of new iRODS versions as additional functionality is added. To hide the physical nature of the $ structure, we adopt a Logical Name Space that can support extensions to the physical structure. The $ Logical Name Space defines a set of "$variables" that map to a value node in the REI structure. This mapping is defined by "data variable mapping" files (files with extensions ".dvm"), which are located in the server/config/reConfigs directory. The $variable mapping defines how the system can translate a $variable name to a path name in the REI structure. For persons implementing Micro-services, iRODS provides "C" functions that allow users to obtain the run-time address of the denoted value. One can have more than one definition for a $variable name. This is needed because different Micro-services might use the same $variables to denote different paths in the REI structure. The function for obtaining values from the REI structure will cycle through these definitions to get to the first non-NULL value. We strongly recommend the use of unique definitions for each $variable, and we advocate that designers use multiple definitions only under very controlled circumstances.

The #variables have a Logical Name Space defined by the attribute set of the iCAT Metadata Catalog. The mappings from #variables to columns in tables in the iCAT schema are defined in lib/core/include/rodsGenQuery.h. These variables can be queried using the generic query call "iquest" available for accessing data from the iCAT database. The command

iquest attrs

lists the persistent state information attributes. In iRODS release 2.1, there are 109 #variables that are associated with data objects, collections, resources, users, monitoring systems, audit trails, and Rules. The #variables and their meaning are listed in Table 4.2.

4.1 SESSION STATE VARIABLES

The $variables can be used as input to a Rule, can also be used to define input to a Micro-service, and can be used to define output from a Micro-service that will be used by subsequent Micro-services. The addition of new variables to the Data Grid requires the recompilation of the software. Thus, an attempt has been made to provide a complete set of variables needed for the management and access of files within a Data Grid. In practice, only a small fraction of these variables is needed for most administrator-modified Rules.The meaning of each $variable is listed in Table 4.1.

Not all Session Variables are available for every action performed in iRODS. Only those Session Variables that are pertinent to a specific action are automatically set. The availability of each Session Variable for Rules listed in the core.irb file depends on the nature of the operation when the Rule is invoked. For example, when the iRODS Server is performing operations on a data object when the Rule is invoked, data object type Session Variables will generally be available for the Micro-services referenced by the Rule.

The msiGetSessionVarValue Micro-service can be used to list all available Session Variables for each Rule into the log file, for example,

acPostProcForRmColl||msiGetSessionVarValue(all,all)|nop.

TABLE 4.1: Session state variables listed in server/config/reConfigs/core.dvm file.	
authStrClient	Authorization string of proxy client (such as DN string)
authStrProxy	Authorization string of proxy user (such as DN string)
backupRescName	Logical resource name
chksum	Checksum (MD5) of the file
collAccess	Access date for a collection
collAccessInx	Internal identifier for access control
collComments	Comment on a collection
collCreate	Creation date for a collection
collExpiry	Expiration date for a collection
collId	Internal Identifier for a collection
collInheritance	Attributes inherited by objects or subcollections: ACL, metadata, pins, locks
collModify	Modification date for a collection
collName	Name of collection
collOwnername	Name of owner of a collection
collParentName	Name of parent collection
connectApiTnx	API that is being used
connectCnt	Pointer to connection structure
connectOption	Type of connection
connectSock	Socket number for connection
connectStatus	Status of connection
dataAccess	Access date of a file
dataAccessInx	Data access identifier (internal)
dataComments	Comments associated with a file
dataCreate	Creation date of a file
dataExpiry	Expiration date for the file
dataId	Internal Identifier for a file
dataModify	Modification date of a file
dataOwner	Owner of the file

TABLE 4.1: (*continued*)

dataOwnerZone	Home Data Grid (zone) of the owner of the file
dataSize	Size of files in bytes
dataType	Data type of the object
destRescName	Logical resource name of the destination for the operation
filePath	Logical path name
freeSpace	Amount of free space on storage resource
freeSpaceTime	Unix time when last free space was computed and registered
freeSpaceTimeStamp	Time stamp information
KVPairs	List of options for a Micro-service, organized as keyword–value pairs
objPath	Physical path name of a file on the logical resource
otherUser	Pointer to other user structure, useful when giving access
otherUserName	Other user name in the form "name@domain"
otherUserType	Role of other user (rodsgroup, rodsadmin, rodsuser, domainadmin, groupadmin, storageadmin, rodscurators)
otherUserZone	Name of the iCAT metadata catalog, or Data Grid, or zone. Unique globally
privClient	iRODS flag that specifies person is an authorized administrator
privProxy	iRODS flag that specifies iRODS proxy for person is an authorized administrator
replNum	Replica number
replStatus	Replica status (0 if up-to-date, 1 if not up-to-date)
rescClass	Class of resource: primary, secondary, archival
rescClassInx	Internal identifier for resource class
rescComments	Comments about resource
rescCreate	Creation date for resource
rescGroupName	Resource group name
rescId	Resource ID
rescInfo	Information about resource
rescLoc	IP address of storage resource
rescMaxObjSize	Maximum file size allowed on storage resource

TABLE 4.1: (*continued*)	
rescModify	Modification date for resource
rescName	Logical resource name
rescType	Type of storage resource: hpss, samfs, database, orb
rescTypeInx	Internal identifier for resource type
rescVaultPath	Physical path name used at storage resource
rodsZoneClient	Name of Data Grid
rodsZoneProxy	Data Grid Zone name of the proxy user
statusString	String for outputting status information
sysUidClient	iRODS user identifier
userAuthSchemeClient	Authorization scheme such as GSI, password, etc.
userAuthSchemeProxy	Type of authentication scheme such as GSI, password
userClient	Pointer to the user client structure
userCommentClient	Comment on user
userCommentProxy	Comment about user
userCreateClient	Pointer to create client structure
userCreateProxy	Pointer to create client structure (not used)
userInfoClient	Tagged information: <EMAIL>user@unc.edu </EMAIL><PHONE>5555555555</PHONE>
userInfoProxy	Tagged information: <EMAIL>user@unc.edu </EMAIL><PHONE>5555555555</PHONE>
userModifyClient	Pointer to modify client structure
userModifyProxy	Pointer to modify client structure (not used)
userNameClient	User name in the form "name@domain"
userNameProxy	Proxy user name in the form "name@domain"
userProxy	Pointer to the structure of the system user who acts as proxy for the client user
version	Version number of the file
writeFlag	Denotes an open is for a read (writeFlag = 0) or for a write (writeFlag = 1)
zoneName	The name of the iCAT instance. This is globally unique.

In Chapter 5.7, the correlation between available Session Variables and the Rules in the default core.irb file is listed. The Session Variables that are automatically available when interactively executing a Rule are also defined.

4.2 PERSISTENT STATE INFORMATION VARIABLES

The system Persistent State Information that is generated by application of Micro-services is stored in the iCAT Metadata Catalog. The iCAT catalog can be queried. The source file

lib/core/include/rodsGenQuery.h

defines the columns available via the General Query interface. Each of the names for a column (metadata attribute or item of state information) begins with 'COL_' (column) for easy identification throughout the source code. The "iquest" client program also uses these field names but without the COL_ prefix.

The #variables are based on a Logical Name Space as defined by the attribute set of the iCAT Metadata Catalog. These variables can be queried using the generic query call "iquest," which is available for accessing data from the iCAT database. The #variables defined within release 2.1 of iRODS are listed in Table 4.2. Executing the command "iquest attrs" will list all of the Persistent State Information Variables.

4.3 USER ENVIRONMENT VARIABLES

Information that defines the preferred user environment is maintained in enviroment variables that are stored on the user's computer. The Environment Variables specify the default data grid that will be accessed, and properties about the user's default collection.

Four Environment Variables are needed by the i-Commands to function:

1. irodsUserName - User name in the iRODS Data Grid
2. irodsHost - Network address of an iRODS Data Grid Server
3. irodsPort - Port number for the data grid metadata catalog (iCAT)
4. irodsZone - Unique identifier for the data grid Zone

Each iRODS Data Grid requires a metadata catalog (iCAT) that is managed as an instance within a database. Since databases can manage multiple instances, we assign a unique port number to each instance. The iRODS Data Grid is therefore completely specified by:

irodsZone : irodsHost : irodsPort

TABLE 4.2: Persistent state variables in the iCAT.

PERSISTENT STATE #VARIABLE	EXPLANATION
AUDIT_ACTION_ID	Internal identifier for type of action that is audited
AUDIT_COMMENT	Comment on audit trail
AUDIT_CREATE_TIME	Creation timestamp for audit trail
AUDIT_MODIFY_TIME	Modification timestamp for audit trail
AUDIT_OBJ_ID	Identifier that starts the range of audit types
AUDIT_USER_ID	User identifier of person requesting operation
COLL_COMMENTS	Comments about the collection
COLL_CREATE_TIME	Collection creation timestamp
COLL_ID	Collection internal identifier
COLL_INHERITANCE	Attributes inherited by subcollections: ACL, metadata, pins, locks
COLL_MODIFY_TIME	Last modification timestamp for collection
COLL_NAME	Logical collection name
COLL_OWNER_NAME	Collection owner
COLL_OWNER_ZONE	Home zone of the collection owner
COLL_PARENT_NAME	Parent collection name
DATA_ACCESS_DATA_ID	Internal identifier of the digital object for which access is defined
DATA_ACCESS_TYPE	Access allowed for the digital object; r, w, x
DATA_ACCESS_USER_ID	User or group for which the access is defined on digital object
DATA_CHECKSUM	Checksum stored as tagged list: <BINHEX>12344</BINHEX><MD5>22234422</MD5>
DATA_COLL_ID	Collection internal identifier
DATA_COMMENTS	Comments about the digital object
DATA_CREATE_TIME	Creation timestamp for the digital object
DATA_EXPIRY	Expiration date for the digital object
DATA_ID	Data internal identifier. A digital object is identified by (zone, collection, data name, replica, version)
DATA_MODIFY_TIME	Last modification timestamp for the digital object

TABLE 4.2: (*continued*)

PERSISTENT STATE #VARIABLE	EXPLANATION
DATA_NAME	Logical name of the digital object
DATA_OWNER_NAME	User who created the object
DATA_OWNER_ZONE	Home zone of the user who created the object
DATA_PATH	Physical path name for digital object in resource
DATA_REPL_NUM	Replica number starting with "1"
DATA_REPL_STATUS	Replica status: locked, is-deleted, pinned, hide
DATA_RESC_GROUP_NAME	Name of resource group in which data are stored
DATA_RESC_NAME	Logical name of storage resource
DATA_SIZE	Size of the digital object in bytes
DATA_STATUS	Digital object status: locked, is-deleted, pinned, hide
DATA_TOKEN_NAMESPACE	Namespace of the data token, e.g., data type
DATA_TYPE_NAME	Type of data: jpeg image, PDF document
DATA_VERSION	Version string assigned to the digital object. Older versions of replicas have a negative replica number
META_COLL_ATTR_ID	Internal identifier for metadata attribute for collection
META_COLL_ATTR_NAME	Metadata attribute name for collection
META_COLL_ATTR_UNITS	Metadata attribute units for collection
META_COLL_ATTR_VALUE	Metadata attribute value for collection
META_DATA_ATTR_ID	Internal identifier for metadata attribute for digital object
META_DATA_ATTR_NAME	Metadata attribute name for digital object
META_DATA_ATTR_UNITS	Metadata attribute units for digital object
META_DATA_ATTR_VALUE	Metadata attribute value for digital object
META_DATA_CREATE_TIME	Time stamp when metadata was created
META_DATA_MODIFY_TIME	Time stamp when metadata was modified
META_NAMESPACE_COLL	Namespace of collection AVU-triplet attribute
META_NAMESPACE_DATA	Namespace of digital object AVU-triplet attribute
META_NAMESPACE_RESC	Namespace of resource AVU-triplet attribute
META_NAMESPACE_USER	Namespace of user AVU-triplet attribute

TABLE 4.2: (*continued*)	
PERSISTENT STATE #VARIABLE	**EXPLANATION**
META_RESC_ATTR_ID	Internal identifier for metadata attribute for resource
META_RESC_ATTR_NAME	Metadata attribute name for resource
META_RESC_ATTR_UNITS	Metadata attribute units for resource
META_RESC_ATTR_VALUE	Metadata attribute value for resource
META_USER_ATTR_ID	Internal identifier for metadata attribute for user
META_USER_ATTR_NAME	Metadata attribute name for user
META_USER_ATTR_UNITS	Metadata attribute units for user
META_USER_ATTR_VALUE	Metadata attribute value for user
RESC_CLASS_NAME	Resource class: primary, secondary, archival
RESC_COMMENT	Comment about resource
RESC_CREATE_TIME	Creation timestamp of resource
RESC_FREE_SPACE	Free space available on resource
RESC_GROUP_NAME	Logical name of the resource group
RESC_GROUP_RESC_ID	Internal identifier for the resource group
RESC_ID	Internal resource identifier
RESC_INFO	Tagged information list: <MAX_OBJ_SIZE>2GBB </MAX_OBJ_SIZE><MIN_LATENCY>1msec </MIIN_LATENCY>
RESC_LOC	Resource IP address
RESC_MODIFY_TIME	Last modification timestamp for resource
RESC_NAME	Logical name of the resource
RESC_TYPE_NAME	Resource type: hpss, samfs, database, orb
RESC_VAULT_PATH	Resource path for storing files
RESC_ZONE_NAME	Name of the iCAT, unique globally
RULE_EXEC_ADDRESS	Host name where the delayed Rule will be executed
RULE_EXEC_ESTIMATED_EXE_TIME	Estimated execution time for the delayed Rule
RULE_EXEC_FREQUENCY	Delayed Rule execution frequency

TABLE 4.2: (*continued*)

PERSISTENT STATE #VARIABLE	EXPLANATION
RULE_EXEC_ID	Internal identifier for a delayed Rule execution request
RULE_EXEC_LAST_EXE_TIME	Previous execution time for the delayed Rule
RULE_EXEC_NAME	Logical name for a delayed Rule execution request
RULE_EXEC_NOTIFICATION_ADDR	Notification address for delayed Rule completion
RULE_EXEC_PRIORITY	Delayed Rule execution priority
RULE_EXEC_REI_FILE_PATH	Path of the file where the context (REI) of the delayed Rule is stored
RULE_EXEC_STATUS	Current status of the delayed Rule
RULE_EXEC_TIME	Time when the delayed Rule will be executed
RULE_EXEC_USER_NAME	User requesting a delayed Rule execution
TOKEN_COMMENT	Comment on token
TOKEN_ID	Internal identifier for token name
TOKEN_NAME	A value in the token namespace; e.g., "gif image"
TOKEN_NAMESPACE	Namespace for tokens; e.g., data type
TOKEN_VALUE	Additional token information string
TOKEN_VALUE2	Additional token information string
TOKEN_VALUE3	Additional token information string
USER_COMMENT	Comment about the user
USER_CREATE_TIME	Creation timestamp
USER_DN	Distinguished name in tagged list: <authType>distinguished Name</authType>
USER_GROUP_ID	Internal identifier for the user group
USER_GROUP_NAME	Logical name for the user group
USER_ID	User internal identifier
USER_INFO	Tagged information: <EMAIL>user@unc.edu</EMAIL> <PHONE>5555555555</PHONE>
USER_MODIFY_TIME	Last modification timestamp

TABLE 4.2: (*continued*)	
PERSISTENT STATE #VARIABLE	**EXPLANATION**
USER_NAME	User name
USER_TYPE	User role (rodsgroup, rodsadmin, rodsuser, domainadmin, group-admin, storageadmin, rodscurators)
USER_ZONE	Home Data Grid or user
ZONE_COMMENT	Comment about the zone
ZONE_CONNECTION	Connection information in tagged list; <PASSWORD>RPS1</PASSWORD> <GSI>DISTNAME</GSI>
ZONE_ID	Data Grid or zone identifier
ZONE_NAME	Data Grid or zone name, name of the iCAT
ZONE_TYPE	Type of zone: local/remote/other

The complete set of i-Commands Environment Variables are:

irodsAuthFileName – The file storing your scrambled password (for authentication)
irodsAuthScheme –Set to GSI for GSI authentication, default is password.
irodsCwd –Your iRODS current working directory
irodsDefResource –A default resource to use when storing (Rules may also apply)
irodsEnvFile – Name of file storing the rest of the Environment Variables
irodsHome – Your iRODS Home collection
irodsHost – An iRODS Server host for the initial connection
irodsPort – The network port (TCP) the server is listening on
irodsServerDn – Used with GSI authentication
irodsUserName – Your iRODS user name
irodsZone – Your iRODS Zone (name of your home iRODS Data Grid)

If you do not provide the irodsHomeEnvironment Variable, it will be set based on the irods-Zone and irodsUserName. If you do not specify the irodsCwd, it will be assumed as irodsHome.

Each of these can be set via a Unix Environment Variable or as a line in a text file, your iRODS environment file. The Environment Variables, if set, override the lines in the environment file.

By default, your iRODS environment file is ~/.irods/.irodsEnv. The install script creates a ~/.irods/.irodsEnv file for the admin account, for example:

irodsHost 'zuri.sdsc.edu'
irodsPort 1378
irodsDefResource=demoResc
irodsHome=/tempZone/home/rods
irodsCwd=/tempZone/home/rods
irodsUserName 'rods'
irodsZone 'tempZone'

You can change ~/.irods/.irodsEnv to some other file by setting the irodsEnvFile Environment Variable. When you do this, a child process will share that environment [and cwd—the current working directory (collection)], which is useful for scripts. By default, without irodsEnvFile set, the cwd will be read by children processes but not by "grandchildren" and beyond; this is so that separate sessions are possible at the same time on the same computer.

• • • •

CHAPTER 5

The iRODS Rule System

iRODS Rules can generally be classified into two Rule Classes:

1. **System level rules**. These are Rules invoked on the iRODS Servers internally to enforce/execute Management Policies for the system. Examples of policies include data management policies such as enforcement of authenticity, integrity, access restrictions, data placement, data presentation, replication, distribution, pre- and post-processing, and metadata extraction and assignment. Other examples are the automation of services such as administration, authentication, authorization, auditing, and accounting. Within the iRODS framework, policy enforcement points have been explicitly defined. Whenever an enforcement point is reached, iRODS invokes the associated policy, which is read from the core .irb file.
2. **User level rules**. The iRODS Rule Engine can also be invoked externally by clients through the irule command or the rcExecMyRule API. Typically, these are workflow-type Rules that allow users to request that the iRODS Servers perform a sequence of operations (Micro-services) on behalf of the user. In addition to providing useful services to users, this type of operation can be very efficient because the operations are done on the servers where the data are located.

Some Rules require immediate execution, whereas others may be executed at a later time in the background (depending on the Rule Execution mode). The *Delayed Execution Service* allows Rules/Micro-services to be queued and executed at a later time by the Rule Execution Server. Examples of Micro-services that are suitable for delayed execution are post-processing operations such as checksuming, replication, and metadata extraction. For example, the post-processing Micro-service msiExtractNaraMetadata was specifically designed to extract and register metadata from National Archives and Records Administration (NARA) Archival Information Locator data objects (NAIL files) that have been uploaded into a NARA collection.

Rules that have been written into a file can be executed through the irule command:
irule –vF Rulename.ir

The irule command has the following input parameters as listed by the help package:
Usage : irule [—test] [-F inputFile] [ruleBody inputParam outParamDesc]

The irule command submits a user-defined Rule to be executed by an iRODS Server. The file containing the Rule must have three lines:

1. ruleBody—This is the body of the Rule to be executed.
2. inputParam—The input parameters used in the Rule are specified in the second line. If there is no input, a string containing "null" must be specified.
3. outParamDesc—Description of the set of output parameters to be returned is specified in the third line. If there is no output, a string containing "null" must be specified.

The format of the ruleBody follows the specification given in Chapter 5.2. The workflow-chain, which is the third part of the Rule body, is a sequence of Micro-services/rules to be executed by this Rule. The Micro-services/Rules in the sequence are separated by the "##" separator.

The input can be specified through the command line or can be read from the .ir file using the -F option. The options on the irule command are:

- -test enable test mode so that the Micro-services are not executed, instead a loopback is performed
- -F inputFile—read the file for the input
- -v verbose
- -h this help

If an inputParam is preceded by the symbol $, the irule command prompts for a new value for the attribute value.

5.1 THE iRODS RULE ARCHITECTURE

At the core of the iRODS Rule System is the iRODS Rule Engine, which runs on all iRODS Servers. The Rule Engine can invoke a number of predefined Micro-services based on the interpretation of the Rule being executed.

The underlying operations that need to be performed are based on C functions that operate on internal C structures. The external view of the execution architecture is based on Actions (typically called tasks) that need to be performed, and external input parameters (called Attributes) that are used to guide and perform these Actions. The C functions themselves are abstracted externally by giving them logical names (we call the functions "internal Micro-services" and the abstractions "external Micro-services"). To make the links between the external world and the internal C apparatus transparent, we define mappings from client libraries to Rules. Moreover, since the operations that are performed by iRODS need to change the Persistent State Information in the ICAT Metadata Catalog, the attributes are mapped to the persistent Logical Name Space for metadata names that are used in the ICAT. The Persistent State Information is listed in Table 4.2.

The foundation for the iRODS architecture is based on the following key concepts, partially discussed in Chapter 4 on ROP:

1. A Persistent Database (#) that shares data (facts) across time and users. Persistent State Information that is maintained in the persistent database is labeled in the following with the symbol #.
2. A Transient Memory ($) that holds data during a session. Session Information that resides in the transient memory is labeled in the following with the symbol $.
3. A set of Actions (T) that name and define the tasks that need to be performed.
4. A set of internal well-defined callable Micro-services (P) made up of procedures and functions that provide the methods for executing the subtasks that need to be performed.
5. A set of external Attributes (A) that is used as a Logical Name Space to externally refer to data and metadata.
6. A set of external Micro-services (M) (or methods) that is used as a Logical Name Space to externally refer to functions that are chained together within a Rule.
7. A set of data variable mappings (DVM) that define a relationship from external Attributes in A to internal elements in # and $.
8. A set of Micro-service name mappings [Function Name Mapping (FNM)] that define a relationship from external Micro-services in M and Actions T to procedures and functions in P and other Action names in T. In a sense, FNM can be seen as providing aliases for Micro-services. One use will be to map different versions of the functions/procedures in P at run time to the actual execution process.
9. A set of Rules (R) that defines what needs to be done for each Action (T) and is based on A and M.

5.2 RULES

A Rule consists of a *name*, *condition*, *workflow-chain*, and *recovery-chain*. A Rule is specified with a line of text that contains these four parts separated by the "|" separator:

actionDef | condition | workflow-chain | recovery-chain

- "actionDef" is the name of the Rule. It is an identifier that can be used by other Rules or external functions to invoke the Rule.

- "condition" is the condition under which this Rule may be executed, that is, this Rule will apply only if the condition is satisfied. Typically, one or more of the session Attributes are used to compose a condition. For example:
  $rescName == demoResc8
  is a condition on the storage resource name. If the storage resource is "demoResc8", then the Rule that uses this condition will be applied. Another example:
  $objPath like /x/y/z/*
  is a condition on the data object or collection path name. The Rule will only be fired if the file in the iRODS Data Grid is underneath the collection /x/y/z.
- "workflow-chain" is the sequence of Micro-services/Rules to be executed by this Rule. The Micro-services/Rules in the sequence are separated by the "##" separator. Each may contain a number of I/O parameters. Note that a Rule can invoke another Rule, or even itself (recursion). If a Rule invokes itself, the designer of the Rule must ensure that the recursion will terminate.
- "recovery-chain" is the set of Micro-services/Rules to be called when execution of any one of the Micro-services/Rules in the workflow-chain fails. The number of Micro-services/Rules in the recovery-chain should be equal to the number in the workflow-chain. If no recovery Action is needed for a given Micro-service/Rule, a "nop" action should be specified. When a Micro-service fails, all of the Micro-services in the "recovery-chain" are executed. Thus, all components within a Rule need to succeed.

5.3 RULE GRAMMAR

The detailed syntactic structure for Rule specification is given in Table 5.1 (alternate definitions are listed under each other).

TABLE 5.1: Rule grammar.

RULE	::= ACTIONDEF | CONDITION | WORKFLOW-CHAIN |RECOVERY-CHAIN
actionDef	::= actionName
	::= actionName(param1, …, paramn)
action	::= actionName
	::= actionName(arg1, …, argn)

TABLE 5.1: (*continued*)			
RULE	**::= ACTIONDEF | CONDITION | WORKFLOW-CHAIN |RECOVERY-CHAIN**		
actionName	::= alpha-numeric string		
Micro-service	::= msName		
	::= msName(arg1, …, argn)		
msName	::= alpha-numeric string		/* pre-defined and compiled */
condition	::=		/* can be empty */
		log-expr	
		(log-expr)	/* parentheses to impose order */
		condition && condition	/* and condition */
		condition !! condition	/* or condition */
log-expr	::= 1		/* true */
	::= 0		/* false */
		expr == expr	
		expr > expr	
		expr < expr	
		expr >= expr	
		expr <= expr	
		expr != expr	/* not equal */
		expr like reg-expr	
		expr not like reg-expr	
expr	::= string		
		number	
		$-variable	/* session variable */
		*-variable	/* state variable */
		concatenation of string, $-variables and/or *-variables	

<table>
<tr><th colspan="3">TABLE 5.1: (continued)</th></tr>
<tr><th>RULE</th><th colspan="2">::= ACTIONDEF | CONDITION | WORKFLOW-CHAIN |RECOVERY-CHAIN</th></tr>
<tr><td>reg-expr</td><td>::= regular-expression-string</td><td></td></tr>
<tr><td>Argx</td><td>::= expr</td><td></td></tr>
<tr><td>paramx</td><td>::= *-variable</td><td></td></tr>
<tr><td></td><td></td><td>number</td></tr>
<tr><td></td><td></td><td>string</td></tr>
<tr><td>workflow-chain</td><td>::= Micro-service</td><td></td></tr>
<tr><td></td><td></td><td>action</td></tr>
<tr><td></td><td></td><td>workflow-chain ##
workflow-chain</td></tr>
<tr><td>recovery-chain</td><td>::= workflow-chain</td><td></td></tr>
</table>

The above syntax defines how Rules can be composed from conditions, state information, session information, and Micro-services. Some sample Rules are:

```
acCreateUser||msiCreateUser##acCreateDefaultCollections##
msiCommit|msiRollback##msiRollback##nop
```

This Rule invokes the following chained Micro-service and Rule:

```
msiCreateUser                 /* execute a Micro-service to create a new user */
acCreateDefaultCollections    /* execute another Rule to create default collections */
msiCommit                     /* register the new state information into the iCAT Metadata
                              Catalog */
```

The corresponding recovery Micro-services are:

```
msiRollback      /* delete user information from the iCAT Metdata Catalog */
msiRollback      /* delete collection information from the iCAT Metadata Catalog */
nop              /* no operation required */
```

A second sample Rule is:

```
acSetRescSchemeForCreate||msiSetDefaultResc(demoResc,noForce)##
msiSetRescSortScheme(random)##msiSetRescSortScheme(byRescType)|
nop##nop##nop
```

This Rule invokes the following chained Micro-services:

msiSetDefaultResc	/* set the default resource if it is available */
msiSetRescSortScheme	/* set random selection of vaults within a storage resource group */
msiSetRescSortScheme	/* set selection of vaults based upon storage type */

The Rule sets three different mechanisms for selecting the location where a file will be created.

The corresponding recovery Micro-services are all nop, meaning no recovery operation is required.

A third example is:

```
acRegisterData|$objPath like
/home/collections.nvo/2mass/*|acGetResource##msiRegisterData##
msiAddACLForDataToUser(2massusers.nvo,write)|nop##
recover_msiRegisterData##
recover_msiAddACLForDataToUser(2massusers.nvo,write)
```

This Rule specifies a condition "$objPath like /home/collections.nov/2mass/*". If the iRODS collection under which the file will be registered includes the path name "/home/collections.nov/2mass/*", then the Rule will be executed. The Rule invokes the following Rule and chained Micro-services:

acGetResource	/* find an acceptable storage location based on the resource selection scheme */
msiRegisterData	/* register a file into the iRODS Data Grid */
msiAddACLForDataToUser	/* give write permission on the file to the user group "2massusers" in the "nvo" project. */

The recovery operations are:

recover_msiRegisterData	/* this Micro-service will delete registration of the file */

recover_msiAddACLForDataToUser /* this Micro-service will delete the ACL for the file */

5.4 RULEGEN LANGUAGE

To make it easier to construct Rules, a rulegen parser has been developed that translates from a higher level Rule language to the grammar specified in Chapter 5.3. The naming convention for the input files to rulegen is that they should have a ".r" extension. The output files created by rulegen should have a ".ir" extension. The grammar for the language of the input files is given in Section 5.4.1 ("Using the RuleGen Parser"). The RuleGen language removes the restriction that the Rule be written in a single line. With RuleGen, each Micro-service can be specified on a separate line, making it easier to create, display, and interpret Rules. The syntax used by the RuleGen language is slightly different from the syntax used by the iRODS Rule Engine. This requires careful attention to specification of inequality tests and quoting of strings (double and single quotes).

All arithmetic operations and inequality test symbols such as (+, *, =) and (<, >) must be written with a preceding space and a following space. All strings used within condition tests that will be parsed in SQL instructions must be quoted using the single quote ('). Strings parsed by rulegen must be quoted using the double quote ("). The choice for the double quote must be the symbol " and not the left (“) or right (”) double quote symbol.

5.4.1 Using the RuleGen Parser

The rulegen parser is created by executing

```
make
```

in the ~/irods/clients/icommands/rulegen directory. A binary file 'rulegen' is created in the ~irods/clients/icommands/bin directory.

The rulegen parser will convert a rulegen input file (".r" extension) into a Rule file (".ir" extension). This is done by running the rulegen parser as shown below:

```
~/irods/clients/icommands/bin/rulegen -s test1.r > test1.ir
```

The output file, test1.ir, can be used as an input file for the irule command.

5.4.2 Example Rule Build

Using the rulegen language, a Rule can be defined in a syntax similar to the C language. The body of the Rule is specified in the brackets after the Rule name "myTestRule". The input parameters are listed as a comma-separated list. The output parameters are listed as a second comma-separated list. An example from the file ~/irods/clients/icommands/rulegen/test2.r is listed below:

```
myTestRule
{
    acGetIcatResults(*Action,*Condition,*B);
    foreach ( *B )
    {
        remote ("andal.sdsc.edu", "null")
        {
            msiDataObjChksum(*B,*Operation,*C);
        }
        msiGetValByKey(*B,DATA_NAME,*D);
        msiGetValByKey(*B,COLL_NAME,*E);
        writeLine(stdout,"CheckSum of *E/*D is *C");
    }
}
```

```
INPUT*Action=chksum,*Condition="COLL_NAME='/tempZone/home/rods/loopTest'",
*Operation = ChksumAll

OUTPUT *Action,*Condition,*Operation,*C,ruleExecOut
```

The INPUT specification is a single line, and the OUTPUT specification is a single line. The *Condition variable that will be used by the acGetIcatResults Rule is specified in double quotes. The string that is used within the *Condition variable to identify the directory name is embedded in single quotes.

This Rule queries the iCAT Metadata Catalog and loops over the result set that is stored in variable "B". For each item in the result set, it calculates a checksum on a remote resource called "andal.sdsc.edu", gets the file name and the collection name from the iCAT catalog, and writes an output line. After running the rulegen program, an iRODS Rule file is generated (listed in ~/irods/clients/icommands/rulegen/test2.ir)

```
myTestRule||acGetIcatResults(*Action,*Condition,*B)##forEachExec(*B,remoteExec(and
al.sdsc.edu,null,msiDataObjChksum(*B,*Operation,*C),nop)##msiGetValByKey(*B,DAT
A_NAME,*D)## msiGetValByKey(*B,COLL_NAME,*E)##writeLine(stdout,CheckSum
of *E/*D is *C),nop##nop##nop##nop)|nop##nop##nop
```

```
*Action = chksum%*Condition = COLL_NAME = '/tempZone/home/rods/loopTest'%*
Operation = ChksumAll
*Action%*Condition%*Operation%*C%ruleExecOut
```

The Rule that is executed by iRODS is written on a single very long line. The input parameters are listed in a second single line at the end of the Rule (no blank lines), followed by the output parameters listed in a third single line. Note that the iteration command "foreach" has been turned into a "forEachExec" Micro-service. Also note that single spaces are required around the "=" sign in the specification of the condition

```
"COLL_NAME = '/tempZone/home/rods/loopTest' "
```

This Rule can be executed by typing

```
irule –vF test2.ir
```

5.5 iRODS RULE ENGINE

The Rule Engine is the interpreter of the Rules in the iRODS system. The Rule Engine can be invoked by any server-side procedure call using the "C" applyRule API.

```
int applyRule(char *inAction, msParamArray_t *inMsParamArray,
      RuleExecInfo_t *rei, int reiSaveFlag)
```

The Rule Engine reads the Rule Base to decide which Rules will apply. First, the Rule Engine selects all the Rules whose Action names are the same as given by the inAction string. These Rules are prioritized based on the order they were added to the Rule Base of the Rule Engine when the iRODS system was started. The first Rule in the list is checked for validation of its condition. If the condition fails, then the next Rule is tried. If no more Rules are available, then the Action fails and a failure status (negative number) is returned to the calling routine. The Micro-services can use the REI structure to pass other failure status and messages. If the condition succeeds, then the Micro-services in the Action chain in the Rule are executed one after the other in a left-to-right order. If all of the Micro-services succeed, then the Action is considered a success and a success status (0) is sent to the calling routine. After successful completion, the inMsParamArray will hold any output values returned by the Rule execution, and the structure REI will reflect any modifications that were made by the Rule execution.

While executing the chain of Micro-services/Actions, if any one of them fails, then the Rule Engine starts a recovery procedure. It applies the corresponding recovery Micro-service or Action defined in the Rule. The recovery for the failed Micro-service/Action is first performed, followed by the recovery of all the previously successful Micro-services/Actions in reverse order. By the time the recovery is completed, the status of the blackboard($) and the persistent database (#) and any side effects should have been rolled back by these recovery procedures. If the calling procedure wants the Rule Engine to recover changes in the REI structure, it can do so by setting the reiSaveFlag. In this case, the Rule Engine will save the REI structure before invoking the first Micro-service/ Action in a Rule and will recover back by resetting the REI structure in case of any Rule failure before invoking any alternate Rules.

Most of the values in the REI structure have a logical name defined for them. We call these names "$variable" names. The mappings from the REI structure to the $variable names can be found in the file "server/config/reConfigs/core.dvm".

The values of $variables can be changed within a Rule. For example, the string $objPath provides the value in the structure rei->doi->objPath. The "assign" Micro-service can change the value of the $variable:

```
assign($objPath, $objPath.Ver0)
```

will add ".Ver0" to the object path. Note that the $variables are accessed during a session. Once you exit from a session by typing "iexit", the $variables will be lost. To make changes permanent, the corresponding information in the iCAT metadata catalog has to be updated (the #variables).

5.6 DEFAULT iRODS RULES

The **core.irb file** contains the Rules that are applied by default when an iRODS Data Grid is created. These Rules are typically modified by the Data Grid Administrator to impose the data Management Policies for the shared collection. For example, the modifications can be specific to a data collection, or to a data type, or to a storage resource, or to a user group.

These Rules can be thought of as policy hooks into the operation of the iRODS Data Grid that enable different policies to be enforced at the discretion of the Data Grid Administrator. There are 69 places where policy can be enforced, typically at the start of a request to create or modify data, collections, users, or resources; or after the end of a request to create or modify data, collections, users, or resources.

Multiple versions of each Rule can be placed in the core.irb file. The Rule listed closest to the top of the core.irb file will be executed first. If the Rule does not meet the required condition or fails, the next version of the Rule will be tried. A generic version of the Rule should be included that will apply if all of the higher priority Rules fail. Note that most of the Rules in the default core.irb file are placeholders that do not execute any Micro-services. The core.irb file (located in the release directory server/config/reConfigs) contains multiple examples of each Rule that have been commented out by inserting a "#" symbol at the beginning of the line.

The names of the default iRODS Rules are listed in Table 5.2. The purpose for each Rule is listed. They can be loosely organized into Rules related to users, resources, collections, data

TABLE 5.2: Default iRODS rules in the core.irb File.

DEFAULT RULES IN CORE.IRB	DESCRIPTION	SESSION VARIABLE SETS
acAclPolicy	Set access rights policy	none
acChkHostAccessControl	Set policy for host access control	
acCreateCollByAdmin	Create a new collection with name "childColl" under the parent collection "parColl"	S1
acCreateDefaultCollections	Create default collections (home, trash)	S1, S6
acCreateUser	Create a new user	S1, S7
acCreateUserF1	Create new user	S1, S6
acCreateUserZoneCollections	Create collections in Data Grid Zone	S1, S6
acDataDeletePolicy	Pre-process for file delete	S1, S3, S4
acDeleteCollByAdmin	Delete the child collection "childColl" under the parent collection "parColl"	S1
acDeleteDefaultCollections	Delete home collection	S1, S7
acDeleteUser	Delete user	S1, S7
acDeleteUserF1	Delete user	S1, S7
acDeleteUserZoneCollections	Delete collections in a Data Grid Zone	S1
acGetIcatResults	Apply the "action" to the list of files that meet the specified condition	
acGetUserByDN	Get userId based on Distinguished Name (in GSI)	S1
acNoChkFilePathPerm	Set policy for checking permissions on registering a file	S1, S3, S4
acPostProcForCollCreate	Post-process for collection create	S1, S5
acPostProcForCopy	Apply processing to file on copy	S1, S3, S4
acPostProcForCreate	Post-process on file create	S1, S3, S4
acPostProcForCreateResource	Post-process on resource creation	S1
acPostProcForCreateToken	Post-process on token creation	S1
acPostProcForCreateUser	Post-process for user create	S1

TABLE 5.2: (*continued*)

DEFAULT RULES IN CORE.IRB	DESCRIPTION	SESSION VARIABLE SETS
acPostProcForDelete	Post-process for file delete	S1, S3, S4
acPostProcForDeleteResource	Post-process on resource deletion	S1
acPostProcForDeleteToken	Post-process on token deletion	S1
acPostProcForDeleteUser	Post-process for user delete	S1
acPostProcForFilePathReg	Post-process for registering a file path	S1, S3, S4
acPostProcForGenQuery	Post-process after general query execution	S1
acPostProcForModifyAccessControl	Post-process for modification of ACLs on data or collection	S1
acPostProcForModifyAVUMetadata	Post-process for modification of AVU metadata for data/collection/resource/user	S1
acPostProcForModifyCollMeta	Post-process on modification of collection metadata	S1, S5
acPostProcForModifyDataObjMeta	Post-process on modification of data metadata	S1, S2
acPostProcForModifyResource	Post-process on resource modification	S1
acPostProcForModifyResourceGroup	Post-process on resource group modification	S1
acPostProcForModifyUser	Post-process for user modify	S1
acPostProcForModifyUserGroup	Post-process for user group modify	S1
acPostProcForObjRename	Post-process for object move	S1, S2
acPostProcForOpen	Post-process for file read or file read. $writeFlag == 0 for open for read, == 1 for open for write	S1, S3, S4
acPostProcForPut	Apply processing to file on put	S1, S3, S4
acPostProcForRmColl	Post-process for collection delete	S1, S5
acPreProcForCollCreate	Pre-process for collection create	S1, S5
acPreProcForCreateResource	Pre-process for resource creation	S1
acPreProcForCreateToken	Pre-process on token creation	S1
acPreProcForCreateUser	Pre-process for user create	S1

TABLE 5.2: *(continued)*

DEFAULT RULES IN CORE.IRB	DESCRIPTION	SESSION VARIABLE SETS
acPreProcForDataObjOpen	Pre-process for file open or read, select which copy of a file to open. $writeFlag == 0 for open for read, == 1 for open for write	S1, S3, S4
acPreProcForDeleteResource	Pre-process on resource deletion	S1
acPreProcForDeleteToken	Pre-process on token deletion	S1
acPreProcForDeleteUser	Pre-process for user delete	S1
acPreProcForGenQuery	Pre-process before general query execution	S1
acPreProcForModifyAccessControl	Pre-process for modification of ACLs on data or collection	S1
acPreProcForModifyAVUMetadata	Pre-process for modification of AVU metadata for data/collection/resource/user	S1
acPreProcForModifyCollMeta	Pre-process on modification of collection metadata	S1, S5
acPreProcForModifyDataObjMeta	Pre-process on modification of data metadata	S1, S2
acPreProcForModifyResource	Pre-process on resource modification	S1
acPreProcForModifyResourceGroup	Pre-process on resource group modification	S1
acPreProcForModifyUser	Pre-process for user modify	S1
acPreProcForModifyUserGroup	Pre-process for user Group modify	S1
acPreProcForObjRename	Pre-process for moving a file	S1, S2
acPreProcForRmColl	Pre-process for collection delete	S1, S5
acPurgeFiles	Purge files satisfying condition on expiration time	
acRenameLocalZone	Rename the Data Grid Zone from the name "oldZone" to the name "newZone"	S1
acSetMultiReplPerResc	Specify number of copies per resource	S1
acSetNumThreads	Set the default number of threads for data transfers	S1
acSetPublicUserPolicy	Set policy for allowed operations by public	S1
acSetRescSchemeForCreate	Pre-process on file create, define selection scheme for default resource	S1, S2

TABLE 5.2: (*continued*)

DEFAULT RULES IN CORE.IRB	DESCRIPTION	SESSION VARIABLE SETS
acSetReServerNumProc	Setting the number of delayed-execution processes to be maintained	S1
acSetVaultPathPolicy	Set policy for assigning physical path name	S1, S3, S4
acTrashPolicy	Set policy for using trash can	S1, S2
acVacuum	Optimize the Postgresql database after waiting "arg1" specified time. See delayExec Micro-service	S1

manipulation, metadata manipulation, and Rule application. Most of the data and metadata manipulation policies can be applied either before an operation within the iRODS framework is executed or after the operation is completed. Typical policies applied before the operation include authorization, resource selection, approval flags, and conversion of input parameters. Typical policies applied after an operation is completed include format transformation, delayed replication, integrity checks, and data subsetting.

5.7 SESSION VARIABLES AVAILABLE FOR EACH RULE

When a policy enforcement point is reached within the iRODS framework, associated Session Variables will be available. The Session Variables may be used within a Rule to decide between options and control the execution of the Rule. Not all Session Variables are available at each policy enforcement point. In particular, note that a limited set of Session Variables are available when Rules are executed interactively.

The available Session Variables can be grouped into seven sets: (1) *SuserAndConn*, (2) *SdataObj1*, (3) *SdataObj2*, (4) *SrescInfo*, (5) *Scollection*, (6) *SuserAdmin1*, and (7) *SuserAdmin2*.

1. The *SuserAndConn* (S1) set contains Session Variables relating to information about the client user and the current client/server connection.This set of Session Variables should be available in all Rules.
2. The *SdataObj1* (S2) set contains just one Session Variable, objPath. It is available in preprocessing Rules before a data object is created.
3. The *SdataObj2* (S3) set contains Session Variables relating to information on a data object.

4. The *SrescInfo* (S4) set contains Session Variables relating to information on an iRODS data storage resource.
5. The *Scollection* (S5) set contains Session Variables relating to information on a Collection.
6. The *SuserAdmin1* (S6) set contains Session Variables relating to information on users for administration purposes.
7. The *SuserAdmin2* (S7) set contains Session Variables for information on new users.

The Session Variables available within each set are listed in Table 5.3.

When Micro-services are executed using the irule command, only the S1 set will be available for the referenced Micro-services. Table 5.2 lists which Session Variable sets are available for use with each of the default iRODS Rules.

TABLE 5.3: Session variables available for use within rules.

$SESSION STATE SET	AVAILABLE $SESSION VARIABLES	$SESSION STATE SET	AVAILABLE $SESSION VARIABLES	$SESSION STATE SET	AVAILABLE $SESSION VARIABLES
S1	authStrClient	S3	backupRescName	S4	freeSpace
S1	authStrProxy	S3	chksum	S4	freeSpaceTimeStamp
S1	connectApiTnx	S3	collId	S4	rescClass
S1	connectCnt	S3	dataAccess	S4	rescClassInx
S1	connectOption	S3	dataAccessInx	S4	rescComments
S1	connectSock	S3	dataComments	S4	rescGroupName
S1	connectStatus	S3	dataId	S4	rescId
S1	otherUser	S3	dataOwner	S4	rescInfo
S1	privClient	S3	dataOwnerZone	S4	rescLoc
S1	privProxy	S3	dataSize	S4	rescMaxObjSize
S1	rodsZoneClient	S3	dataType	S4	rescName
S1	rodsZoneProxy	S3	destRescName	S4	rescType
S1	userAuthScheme Client	S3	filePath	S4	rescTypeInx
S1	userAuthSchemeProxy	S3	objPath	S4	rescVaultPath
S1	userNameClient	S3	replNum	S4	zoneName

TABLE 5.3: (*continued*)

$ SESSION STATE SET	AVAILABLE $ SESSION VARIABLES	$ SESSION STATE SET	AVAILABLE $ SESSION VARIABLES	$ SESSION STATE SET	AVAILABLE $ SESSION VARIABLES
S1	userNameProxy	S3	replStatus		
		S3	statusString	S5	collName
S2	objPath	S3	version	S5	collParentName
		S3	writeFlag		
				S6	otherUserName
				S6	otherUserZone
				S6	otherUserType
				S7	otherUserName
				S7	otherUserZone

• • • •

CHAPTER 6

iRODS Micro-services

Micro-services are small, well-defined procedures/functions that perform a simple task. Micro-services are developed and made available by system programmers and application programmers and compiled into the iRODS Server code. Users and administrators can chain these Micro-services to implement a function that they want to use or provide for others. In this manner, the users/administrators can have full control over what happens when one performs a macro-level functionality. These macro-level functionalities are called Actions. By having more than one chain of Micro-services for an Action, a system can have multiple ways of performing the Action. Using priorities and validation conditions at run-time, the system chooses the "best" Micro-service chain to be executed. There are other caveats to this execution paradigm that were discussed in Chapter 4.

The task performed by a Micro-service can be quite small or very involved. We leave it to the Micro-service developer to choose the proper level of granularity for their task differentiation. A good rule of thumb is to divide a large task into subtasks with well-defined interfaces and make each into a Micro-service. If two such subtasks are always done together, it would be a good idea to group them together into one Micro-service. Since the user/administrator chains the Micro-services into Actions, having too fine-grained a differentiation will make the splicing cumbersome and difficult. On the other hand, making a large task into a single Micro-service takes away the control that is given to the end user/administrator, who might want to choose not to do some parts of the task. We recommend that normal coding practices and good design principles used in Module and method generation be applied in deciding the granularity for each Micro-service task.

The Micro-services are organized into the following categories:

- Core Micro-services—Functions for Rule Engine control, Workflow creation, Data Object Low-level manipulation, Higher-level Data Object.
- iCAT Services—Functions for manipulating System metadata, and for interacting with the iCAT Metadata Catalog.
- Framework Services—Functions for Rule-oriented remote database access, high-performance Xmessaging system message passing, sending e-mail, manipulating Keyword–Value attribute pairs, supporting User-defined services, and supporting System level services.

- Module Micro-services—Sets of functions developed for specific communities, for example, the ERA (Electronic Records Archives) Program at NARA, eXtensible Markup Language (XML) manipulation, Hierarchical Data Format (HDF) manipulation, image property manipulation, Web service interaction, the French National Library, etc.

Within each category, multiple Micro-services may be defined. The list continues to grow over time as more functionality is added to the iRODS Data Grid. In version 2.1 of iRODS, 185 Micro-services have been implemented. They are listed in Tables 6.1 through 6.18. The Rule Engine Micro-services are used to modify the Rule Base and display the currently loaded Rules. The mappings from the Session Variable names (DVM) and the Micro-service names (FNM) can also be modified. The FNM maps the name of the Micro-service to the C function that implements the associated operations.

The iRODS Data Grid encapsulates all workflow mechanisms such as loops, conditions, and flow control as Micro-services. This minimizes the complexity of the workflow language, while enabling sophisticated workflows to be implemented. The same approach is used in client-side workflow systems such as Taverna and Kepler. When a query is made on the iCAT Metadata

TABLE 6.1: Rule engine micro-services.

RULE ENGINE MICRO-SERVICES	DESCRIPTION
msiAdmAddAppRuleStruct	Adds application-level IRB Rules and DVM and FNM mappings to the Rule Engine
msiAdmAppendToTopOfCoreIRB	Pre-pends another irb file to the core.irb file
msiAdmChangeCoreIRB	Changes the core.irb file from the client
msiAdmClearAppRuleStruct	Clears application-level IRB Rules and DVM and FNM mappings that were loaded into the Rule Engine
msiAdmShowDVM	Displays the currently loaded variable name mappings
msiAdmShowFNM	Displays the currently loaded microServices/ Actions name mappings
msiAdmShowIRB	Displays the currently loaded Rules

TABLE 6.2: Workflow micro-services.

WORKFLOW MICRO-SERVICES	DESCRIPTION
applyAllRules	Apply all applicable Rules when executing a given Rule
assign	Assign a value to a parameter
break	Breaks out of While, For, and forEach loops
cut	Not to retry any other applicable Rules for this action
delayExec	Delays an execution of Micro-services or Rules
fail	Fail immediately recovery and retries are possible
forEachExec	For loop iterating over a row of tables or a list
forExec	For loop with initial, step, and end condition
ifExec	If-then-else conditional branch
msiGoodFailure	Useful when you want to fail but no recovery initiated
msiSleep	Sleep
nop, null	No action
remoteExec	Remote execution of Micro-services or Rules
succeed	Succeed immediately
whileExec	While loop
writeLine	Writes a line (with endofline) to stdout buffer
writeString	Writes a string to stdout buffer

Catalog, a list of files that satisfy that query is generated. The "forEachExec" Micro-service loops over the output list, enabling a specified workflow to be applied to each file in the list. The "assign" Micro-service enables initialization of Session Variables and arithmetic on Session Variables. The "ifExec" Micro-service enables testing of Session Variable values, and the conditional execution of workflows.

TABLE 6.3: Data object low-level micro-services (can be called by client through irule).

DATA OBJECT LOW LEVEL MICRO-SERVICE	DESCRIPTION (CAN BE CALLED BY CLIENT THROUGH IRULE)
msiDataObjClose	Close an opened data object
msiDataObjCreate	Create a data object
msiDataObjLseek	Lseek
msiDataObjOpen	Open a data object
msiDataObjRead	Read an opened data object
msiDataObjWrite	Write

The Micro-services for the low-level manipulation of data objects correspond to standard Posix I/O operations. A file can be opened, read or written, and closed. For partial reads on a file, an Lseek can be done to the correct location within the file.

Higher-level data and collection operations correspond to manipulation of objects (files). A file can be put into the iRODS Data Grid (msiDataObjPut Micro-service), or read from the Data Grid (msiDataObjGet Micro-service). A file can be copied between subcollections (msiDataObjCopy). Or it can be physically moved to another storage location (msiDataObjPhymv). A file can be replicated (msiDataObjRepl). In this case, an additional physical copy is made. A file in a remote storage location can be registered into the data grid (msiPhyPathReg). Operations on files include setting access controls, creating checksums, renaming, and deleting. Deletion of a file corresponds to a logical move into a trashcan collection.

Collections can be created, replicated, and deleted.

The Micro-services provided by iRODS are written in C and installed with the iRODS Server at each storage location. This makes it possible to tightly control the functions that are executed at each storage location, and ensure a consistent operation. In addition, iRODS supports the invocation of remote commands to run applications that have been installed outside of iRODS at the remote storage location.

Micro-services are provided for managing the iCAT catalog. If a PostgreSQL database is used to hold the iCAT catalog, periodic "vacuum" operations need to be applied to remove deleted information. The msiVacuum Micro-service initiates the PostgreSQL vacuum operation.

TABLE 6.4: Data object and collection micro-services (can be called by client through irule).

DATA OBJECT MICRO-SERVICES	DESCRIPTION (CAN BE CALLED BY CLIENT THROUGH IRULE)
msiCheckOwner	Check whether user is owner
msiCheckPermission	Check whether permission is granted
msiDataObjChksum	Checksum a data object
msiDataObjCopy	Copy
msiDataObjGet	Get
msiDataObjPhymv	Move a data object from one resource to another
msiDataObjPut	Put
msiDataObjPutWithOptions	Put with options
msiDataObjRename	Rename a data object
msiDataObjRepl	Replicate
msiDataObjRsync	Rsync a data between iRODS and local file
msiDataObjTrim	Trim the replica
msiDataObjUnlink	Delete
msiGetObjType	Finds if a given value is a data, coll, resc, . . .
msiObjStat	Stat an object
msiPhyPathReg	Register a physical file into iRODS Data Grid
COLLECTION MICRO-SERVICES	
msiCollCreate	Create a collection
msiCollRepl	Replicate all files in a collection
msiRmColl	Delete a collection

TABLE 6.5: Proxy command micro-services and Web services.

PROXY COMMAND MICRO-SERVICES	DESCRIPTION
msiExecCmd	Remotely execute a command
WEB SERVICES	
msiConvertCurrency	Returns conversion rate for currencies from one country to another, using Web service provided by http://www.webserviceX.NET
msiGetQuote	Returns a stock quotation using Web service provided by http://www.webserviceX.NET
msiIp2location	Returns host name and details given an IP address, using the Web service provided by http://ws.fraudlabs.com/
msiObjByName	Returns position and type of an astronomical object given a name using the NASA/IPAC Extragalactic Database (NED) Web service at http://voservices.net/ws_v2_0/NED.asmx
msiSdssImgCutout_GetJpeg	Returns an image buffer given a position andcutout size using the SDSS Image Cut Out Web service at http://skyserver.sdss.org

The iCAT catalog holds system information about users, files, collections, resources, and Rules. In addition to Micro-services for manipulating properties about users, collections, and zones, iRODS provides functions to make a query, and then execute the query. When a query is made,

ICAT SYSTEM MICRO-SERVICES	DESCRIPTION
msiVacuum	PostgreSQL vacuum done periodically

iRODS constructs the "SQL" that will be issued to the iRODS Metadata Catalog. When the query is executed, iRODS returns a list of files (or users or collections or resources) that satisfy the query. Each item in the result list can then be manipulated and processed by additional Micro-services by using the "forEachExec" Micro-service. Note that the maximum length of the list is 500 items. To retrieve information about the second set of 500 items in a large query result, the "msiGetMoreRows" Micro-service is used.

ICAT MICRO-SERVICES	DESCRIPTION
msiAddUserToGroup	Adds a user to a group
msiCommit	Commit the database transaction
msiCreateCollByAdmin	Create a collection by administrator
msiCreateUser	Create a new user
msiDeleteCollByAdmin	Delete a collection by administrator
msiDeleteUser	Delete a user
msiExecGenQuery	Executes a given general query structure and returns results
msiExecStrCondQuery	Given a condition string creates an iCAT query, executes it, and returns the values
msiGetMoreRows	Continues an unfinished query, calls msiExecStrCondQuery, and returns results
msiMakeGenQuery	Combines msiMakeQuery and msiExecGenQuery and returns the results of the execution
msiMakeQuery	Given a select list and a condition list, creates a pseudoSQL query
msiRenameCollection	Renames a collection; used via a Rule with above msiRenameLocalZone
msiRenameLocalZone	Renames the local zone by updating various tables
msiRollback	Roll back the database transaction

The iRODS Data Grid can issue commands against a remote database. Currently, the remote database is assumed to be the same as the database that holds the iCAT Metadata Catalog. The operations that can be performed on the remote database include execution of SQL operations, updates to metadata, and formatting of results. The result of the operation can be ignored (not returned), or written to standardout, or written into an iRODS data object.

RULE-ORIENTED DATABASE ACCESS MICROSERVICES	DESCRIPTION
msiRdaCommit	Commit Changes to the database.
msiRdaNoResults	Performs an SQL operation on a remote database but without returning resulting output.
msiRdaRollback	Rollback (don't commit) changes to the database.
msiRdaToDataObj	Stores results in an iRODS dataObject
msiRdaToStdout	Calls new RDA functions to interface to an arbitrary database returning results in standardout.

The iRODS Data Grid provides a high-performance messaging system for sending messages between iRODS Servers. The communication between servers can be driven by explicit Micro-services to create a message stream connection, create a packet, send a packet, receive a packet, and disconnect from the Xmessage Server.

XMESSAGING SYSTEM MICRO-SERVICES	DESCRIPTION
msiCreateXmsgInp	Creates an Xmsg packet, given required information
msiRcvXmsg	Receives an Xmsg packet
msiSendXmsg	Sends an Xmsg packet
msiXmsgCreateStream	Creates a new Message Stream
msiXmsgServerConnect	Connects to the XMessage Server designated by an iRODS Environment file variable
msiXmsgServerDisConnect	Disconnects from the Xmessage Server

The iRODS Data Grid can send messages through e-mail. A message can be composed and sent, or the information that has been written to the REI standardout structure can be sent.

EMAIL MICRO-SERVICES	DESCRIPTION
msiSendMail	Sends email!
sendStdoutAsEmail	Sends rei stdout as email

A standard way to load metadata into an iRODS Data Grid is to construct a file that lists keyword–value–unit triplets. For each keyword name, the value and unit are specified, along with the file name to which the attributes will be assigned. A structure in memory holds the information when queries are made on the iCAT catalog. Micro-services are provided to extract the value from the memory structure, write the values to standardout, ingest the metadata into the iCAT catalog, and remove attributes from the iCAT catalog. The format of the keyword–value pairs can be converted into "%" delimited strings.

KEYVALUE (ATTRVALUE) MICRO-SERVICES	DESCRIPTION
msiAssociateKeyValuePairsToObj	Ingest object metadata into iCAT from an AVU structure
msiGetValByKey	Given a key and a keyValPair struct, extract the corresponding value
msiPrintKeyValPair	Print keyvalue pairs to rei stdout buffer
msiRemoveKeyValuePairsFromObj	Remove object metadata from iCAT using an AVU structure
msiStrArray2String	Array of strings converted to a string separated by % signs
msiString2KeyValPair	Convert a %-separated keyvalue pair strings into keyValPair structure
writeKeyValPairs	Write keyword value pairs to stdout or stderr, using the given separator

User-level Micro-services support interactive use of the iRODS Data Grid. The types of functions range from retrieval and formatting of the system time, to loading metadata from a file, to writing a buffer to standardout, to writing an integer to standardout.

USER MICRO-SERVICES	DESCRIPTION
msiApplyDCMetadataTemplate	Adds Dublin Core metadata fields to an object or collection
msiExtractNaraMetadata	Extracts NARAstyle metadata from AVU triplets
msiExtractTemplateMDFromBuf	Extracts AVU information using a template
msiFreeBuffer	Frees a buffer in an inOutStruct
msiGetDiffTime	Returns the difference between two system timestamps, given in Unix format (stored in a string)
msiGetIcatTime	Returns the system time of the iCAT Server
msiGetSystemTime	Returns the local system time of an iRODS Server
msiGetTaggedValueFromString	Given a TagName gets the value from a file in taggedformat (pseudoXML)
msiHumanToSystemTime	Converts a human readable date to a system timestamp
msiLoadMetadataFromFile	Loads AVU metadata from a file
msiReadMDTemplateInto TagStruct	Load template file contents into Tag structure
writeBytesBuf	Writes the buffer in an inOutStruct to stdout or stderr
writePosInt	Writes an integer to stdout or stderr

The iRODS Data Grid has system level Micro-services that can only be called by the server process. These Micro-services cannot be invoked using the interactive "irule" command. The functions that are supported include setting access controls, turning off the ability to delete files, setting the default location where data will be written, specifying the number of parallel I/O streams to be used for transferring large files, and restricting the operations that can be executed by a "public" user.

SYSTEM MICRO-SERVICES	DESCRIPTION (CAN ONLY BE CALLED BY THE SERVER PROCESS)
msiCheckHostAccessControl	Sets the access control policy
msiDataObjChksum	Checksum a data object
msiDeleteDisallowed	Set the policy for determining certain data cannot be deleted
msiNoChkFilePathPerm	Do Not Check file path permission when registering
msiNoTrashCan	Set the policy to No trash can
msiSetDataObjAvoidResc	Specify the Copy to avoid
msiSetDataObjPreferredResc	If the data has multiple copies, specify the preferred Copy to use
msiSetDataTypeFromExt	Get data type based on file name extension
msiSetDefaultResc	Set the default resource
msiSetGraftPathScheme	Set the scheme for composing the physical path in the vault to GRAFT_PATH
msiSetMultiReplPerResc	Sets the number of copies per resource to unlimited
msiSetNoDirectRescInp	Sets a list of resources that cannot be used by a normal user directly
msiSetNumThreads	Specify the parameters for determining the number of threads to use for data transfer
msiSetPublicUserOpr	Sets a list of operations that can be performed by the user "public"
msiSetRandomScheme	Set the scheme for composing the physical path in the vault to RANDOM
msiSetRescSortScheme	Set the scheme for selecting the best resource to use
msiSetResource	Sets the resource from default
msiSortDataObj	Sort the replica randomly when choosing which Copy to use
msiStageDataObj	Stage the data object to the specified resource before operation
msiSysReplDataObj	Replicate a data object

The iRODS Data Grid supports the organization of Micro-services into Modules. The iRODS Data Grid administrator specifies which Modules will be loaded at each iRODS Server. Separate Modules have been created for Micro-services used by the NARA Transcontinental Persistent Archive Prototype, for manipulation of XML files (this requires installation of libxml and libxslt), for executing the HDF version 5 libraries, for managing properties of image files, and for the French National Library. The Modules can be loaded together, or subsets of the Modules can be installed. In Chapter 8, instructions are provided for creating Modules of Micro-services, and for adding a Micro-service to a Module.

The NARA Transcontinental Persistent Archive Prototype uses Micro-services to manipulate the hierarchical metadata associated with the Life Cycle Data Requirements Guide, parse audit trails, extract and load lists of access controls, extract and load user-defined metadata, and replicate collections. These functions are needed to implement trusted repository assessment criteria.

NARA TRANSCONTINENTAL ARCHIVE	DESCRIPTION
msiCopyAVUMetadata	Copies metadata triplets from an iRODS object to another iRODS object
msiCreateUserAccountsFromDataObj	Creates new user from information in an iRODS data object
msiDeleteUsersFromDataObj	Deletes user based on information in an iRODS data object
msiExportRecursiveCollMeta	Exports metadata AVU triplets for a collection and its contents in a "|" separated format
msiGetAuditTrailInfoByActionID	Retrieves Audit Trail information for a given action ID
msiGetAuditTrailInfoByKeywords	Retrieves Audit Trail information by keywords in the comment field
msiGetAuditTrailInfoByObjectID	Retrieves Audit Trail information for an object ID
msiGetAuditTrailInfoByTimeStamp	Retrieves Audit Trail information by time stamp period
msiGetAuditTrailInfoByUserID	Retrieves Audit Trail information for a user ID

(*continued*)	
NARA TRANSCONTINENTAL ARCHIVE	**DESCRIPTION**
msiGetCollectionACL	Gets ACL (Access Control List) for a collection in "|" separated format
msiGetCollectionContentsReport	Returns the object count and total disk usage of a collection
msiGetCollectionPSmeta	Retrieves metadata AVU triplets for a collection in "|" separated format
msiGetDataObjACL	Gets ACL (Access Control List) for a data object in "|" separated format
msiGetDataObjAIP	Gets the Archival information Package of a data object in XML format
msiGetDataObjAVUs	Retrieves metadata AVU triplets for a data object and returns them As an XML file
msiGetDataObjPSmeta	Retrieves metadata AVU triplets for a data object in "|" separated format
msiGetUserACL	Gets user ACL for all objects and collections
msiGetUserInfo	Gets information about user
msiGuessDataType	Guesses the data type of an object based on its file extension
msiLoadACLFromDataObj	Loads ACL from information in a iRODS data object
msiLoadMetadataFromDataObj	Parses an iRODS object for new metadata AVUs
msiLoadUserModsFromDataObj	Modifies user information from information in a iRODS data object
msiRecursiveCollCopy	Recursively copies a collection and its contents including metadata
msiSetDataType	Sets data type for an object

The iRODS Data Grid can apply an Extensible Stylesheet Language Transformation (XSLT) to an XML file, and store the resulting file in the iRODS Data Grid.

XML	DESCRIPTION
msiXsltApply	Given an XML object and an XSLT object, returns the XML object after applying the XSLT transformation

HDF is used to package scientific data into containers (files). HDF libraries are invoked by the iRODS server at the remote storage location to extract files from the HDF container, read data from a file, and read data attributes.

HDF	DESCRIPTION
msiH5Dataset_read	Read data from and HDF file
msiH5Dataset_read_attribute	Read data attribute from an HDF file
msiH5File_close	Close an HDF file
msiH5File_open	Open an HDF file
msiH5Group_read_attribute	Read attributes of a group in an HDF file

Images contain metadata that describe the type of image, how the image was created, and the properties of the image. In order to manipulate an image, the properties are extracted from the image. A generic set of Micro-services has been developed to support manipulation of a set of properties.

PROPERTIES	DESCRIPTION
msiPropertiesAdd	Add a property and value to a property list. If the property is already in the list, its value is changed. Otherwise the property is added.
msiPropertiesClear	Clear a property list.
msiPropertiesClone	Clone a property list, returning a new property list.

(*continued*)

PROPERTIES	DESCRIPTION
msiPropertiesExists	Return true (integer 1) if the keyword has a property value in the property list, and false (integer 0) otherwise. The property list is unmodified.
msiPropertiesFromString	Parse a string into a new property list. The existing property list, if any, is deleted.
msiPropertiesGet	Get the value of a property in a property list. The property list is left unmodified.
msiPropertiesNew	Create a new empty property list.
msiPropertiesRemove	Remove a property from the list.
msiPropertiesSet	Set the value of a property in a property list. If the property is already in the list, its value is changed. Otherwise, the property is added.
msiPropertiesToString	Convert a property list into a string buffer. The property list is left unmodified.

The French National Library created a Micro-service to format the system time.

FRENCH NATIONAL LIBRARY	DESCRIPTION
msiGetFormattedSystemTime	Returns the local system time

Although Micro-services can be any normal C procedure, there is a standard template that needs to be used when making a C procedure into a Micro-service. The standard template provides the in-memory structures that are used to pass data between Micro-services, a mechanism to check interactions between Micro-services, and standard error returns. A C procedure that you want to turn into a Micro-service can have any number of arguments and any type or structure (with some caveats, see discussion on the parameter structure). When the Rule Engine interacts with a Micro-service, it interacts with a published (standardized within iRODS) parametric structure of the type called msParam_t. Hence, glue code is needed that converts from msParam_t to the actual argument types of the underlying Micro-service. We call this glue code a Micro-service interface (msi for short). The msi routine will map the msParam_t structure to the call arguments and convert back any output parameters to the msParam_t structure. We illustrate with an example below.

We recommend that the Micro-service interface procedures be pre-fixed with the three-letter acronym msi. Hence, a procedure called createCollection can have an interface routine called msiCreateCollection. The Rule Engine will invoke msiCreateCollection that, in turn, will invoke createCollection.

Each of the msi procedure calls is registered in the Rule Engine. Only these registered Micro-services can be invoked by the Rule Engine. The registration is done by adding the name of the msi procedure call to a C structure table maintained for this purpose. The table is called Action-Table[] and is found in the server/include/reAction.h file.

6.1 MICRO-SERVICE INPUT/OUTPUT ARGUMENTS

One can pass arguments to a Rule, Micro-service, or Action through explicit arguments, as done in the case of C function or procedure calls. The input parameters can take two forms:

- **Literal**—If an argument does not begin with a special character (#, $, or *), it is treated as a character string input. For example, in the Micro-service msiSetRescSortScheme (random), the character string "random" will be passed in as input. Literals can only be used as input parameters and not output parameters.
- **Variable**—If an argument begins with the * character, it is treated as a variable argument. Variable arguments can be used both as input and output parameters. The output parameter from one Micro-service can be explicitly specified as the input parameter of another Micro-service. This powerful capability allows very complex workflow-like Rules to be constructed. For example, in the following workflow chain:

  msiDataObjOpen(/x/y/z,*FD)##msiDataObjRead(*FD,10000,*BUF)

  msiDataObjOpen opens a data object with the input path /x/y/z and the output file descriptor is placed in the variable parameter *FD. *FD is then used by msiDataObjRead as an input parameter for the read.

User-level workflow-like Rules can be invoked through the irule command or the rcExecMyRule API. Internally, the Rule system uses the msParam_t structure to store the content of Variable arguments. The definition of the structure can be found in the file clientLib/include/api/dataObjInpOut.h.

```
typedef struct MsParam {
   char *label;
   char *type;        /* this is the name of the packing instruction in * rodsPackTable.h */
```

```
    void *inOutStruct;
    bytesBuf_t *inpOutBuf;
} msParam_t;
```

This data structure is universal in the sense that it can be used to represent all parameter types, including very complex data structures. The field label is the identifier used in the actual Rule. That is, if a Rule calls the Micro-service msiDataObjCreate(*A,*S_FD), the strings "*A" and "*S_FD" are the labels of their respective structures. The type field identifies the type of data that is stored in the inOutStruct. The data types suppported, although fairly extensive, are restricted to the ones that are given in the file clientLib/include/api/rodsDef.h. The set of supported data types and structures is listed in Table 6.2. The value of I/O is specified in the inOutStruct field. The inpOutBuf is a buffer that can be used to pass binary data as part of the parameter. The parameters are passed as an array as defined in the following type definition.

```
typedef struct MsParamArray {
  int len;
  int oprType;
  msParam_t msParam;
} msParamArray_t;
```

The msParam_t structure provides a uniform type definition for the Rule Engine to handle and operate. The set of supported types is listed in Table 6.6. The data structures include support for passing parameters for Rule invocation using the msParam structure and for passing values between client–server and server–server interactions. The values can be found in the file clientLib/include/rodsPackTable.h.

TABLE 6.6: Data structures supported by iRODS.

STRUCTURE	USE
AuthInfo_PI	*Authentication information*
BytesBuf_PI	*Data buffer*
CollInfo_PI	*Collection information*
DataObjInfo_PI	*Data object information*
DataOprInp_PI	*Data object information from client*

TABLE 6.6: (*continued*)

STRUCTURE	USE
GenQueryInp_PI	*General query input*
GenQueryOut_PI	*General query output*
INT_PI	*Integer variable*
InxIvalPair_PI	*Indexed integer list*
InxValPair_PI	*Indexed string list*
KeyValPair_PI	*Keyword value pairs*
MsParam_PI	*Micro-service parameters*
MsParamArray_PI	*Micro-service arrays*
PortalOprOut_PI	*Communication portal operation structure*
PortList_PI	*List of communication ports*
ReArg_PI	*Action arguments*
Rei_PI	*Rule execution infrastructure*
ReiAndArg_PI	*Combination of above two argument structures*
RErrMsg_PI	*Rule error messages*
RError_PI	*Rule error*
RescGrpInfo_PI	*Resource group information*
RHostAddr_PI	*Remote host address*
RODS_DIRENT_T_PI	*Directory entry information*
RODS_STAT_T_PI	*File or directory stat information*
SqlResult_PI	*Table structure returned by running an iCAT query*
StartupPack_PI	*Initial client-server handshake*
STR_PI	*String variable*
TransStat_PI	*A structure standardized for mapping stats for various file systems*
UserInfo_PI	*User information*
UserOtherInfo_PI	*Second user information structure*
Version_PI	*Software version structure*

The inOutStruct tells the iRODS Data Grid where the value defined by the input structure is located. The inOutStuct is a pointer to the value of the input structure being passed. It can be null. The inpOutBuf is used to hold any binary buffers that need to be passed as part of the argument.

6.2 NAMING CONVENTIONS

When adding files and functions, we recommend standard naming conventions for ease of maintenance. Naming conventions are useful for helping maintain the programs and functions that are created under iRODS. Even though we do not force these conventions on developers, we recommend their usage for maintaining good programming practice.

6.2.1 Variable Naming Conventions

We recommend that:

- Variable names use multiple descriptive words.
  Example: myRodsArgs
- Variable names use camel-case to distinguish words, with the first letter of each word component capitalized:
  Example: genQueryInp

6.2.2 Constant Naming Conventions

We recommend using one of the two following conventions:

- Constant string names use multiple descriptive words and start with an uppercase letter.
  Example: Msg_Header_PI
- Constant string names use uppercase letters separated with an underscore.
  Example: NAME_LEN

6.2.3 Function Naming Conventions

All C functions in iRODS occupy the same namespace. To avoid function name collisions, we recommend that:

- Function names use multiple descriptive words.
  Example: getMsParamByLabel
- Function names use camel-case to distinguish words:
  Example: printMsParam

- Micro-service function names start with "msi":
  Example: msiDataObjGet
- Micro-service helper function names start with "mh":
- Server function names start with "rs".
- Client function names start with "rc".

6.2.4 File Naming Conventions

The purpose of a file may be inferred by the location of the file in the iRODS directory tree. For instance, those in the server/re/src directory are part of the Rule Engine, whereas those in the clients/icommands/src directory are command-line tools. Beyond this, we recommend that:

- File names use multiple descriptive words.
  Example: rodsServer.c contains the iRODS Server main program.
- File names reflect the names of functions in the file.
  Example: msParam.c contains utility functions that work with the msParam structure.
- File names use camel-case to distinguish words:
  Example: irodsReServer.c

No two files in the same directory may have names that differ only by case. Case-sensitive names cause problems with Windows and the old Mac file systems.

• • • •

CHAPTER 7

Example Rules

Many types of Rules can be created that automate an administrative task, or that validate an assessment criteria, or that enforce an administrative policy. Example Rules are provided to illustrate types of actions that can be performed as server-side workflows at remote storage locations. In the iRODS distribution, the directory irods/clients/icommands/test holds multiple Rule examples. This chapter describes the construction of the Rules, the Micro-services that are used to compose the Rule, and the results from application of the Rule. A description of how the Rule can be invoked from the command line using the irule Unix command is also given.

We organize the example Rules into five classes:

1. File manipulation
2. System testing
3. User interaction
4. Rule manipulation
5. Resource setting

In the rest of this chapter, the Rules are pretty-printed using the Rulegen language (*.r). The original Rules can be found in their respective *.ir files in the clients/icommands/test directory in the iRODS release. Since none of the Micro-services here have recovery equivalents, they are ignored in the pretty printing. When typing in the Rules, pay careful attention to the character used for the double quote. Note that several text editors use alternate characters for the double quote.

(“, ”, ")

The required value is ". You may have to replace your text editor's character for the double quote for rulegen to work correctly.

To specify no input arguments in rulegen, use

INPUT *A=null

7.1 FILE MANIPULATION RULES

7.1.1 List All Files in a Collection

The "listColl.ir" Rule queries the iCAT Metadata Catalog and retrieves a list of files that satisfy a specified "Condition". An "Action" specifies the operation that is performed upon the files as they are added to the list. Each file that is manipulated is printed to "stdout", followed by the printing of a separator line.

The file called listColl.ir contains the body of the Rule and a specification of the input parameters. The Rule syntax appropriate for the rulegen Rule generator is listed below. Running the rulegen utility on this list will create the Rule contained in the listColl.ir file. Note that the input parameters in the line starting with "INPUT" are actually listed on a single line.

```
myTestRule(*Action, *Condition)
{
        acGetIcatResults(*Action,*Condition,*B);
        foreach ( *B )
        {
          msiPrintKeyValPair(stdout,*B);
                writeLine(stdout,*K);
        }
}
INPUT *Action=list,*Condition="COLL_NAME = '/tempZone/home/rods/loopTest' ",
*K="-------------------------"
OUTPUT *Action, ruleExecOut
```

The "listColl.ir" Rule invokes the Micro-services:

1. acGetIcatResults—A Rule that, given an "Action" and an SQL "Condition", returns a table of values. In this case:

"Action":	is the "list" command
"Condition":	limits application to a specific Collection name, COLL_NAME = '/tempZone/home/rods/loopTest' (other conditions can be specified)

2. foreach—A rulegen name for the forEachExecMicro-service that takes a table (or list of strings, or %-separated string list), and for each item in the list, executes the corresponding body of the for-loop. The first parameter in the forEachExec Micro-services specifies

the variable that has the list (the same variable name is used in the body of the loop to denote an item of the list!). The second parameter in forEachExec is the sequence of Micro-services contained in the braces after the rulegen foreach command. The sequence will be executed for each item in the list. The third parameter in forEachExec is the recovery Micro-service sequence.

3. msiPrintKeyValPair—A Micro-service that prints a row in a table as a set of key-value pairs to 'stdout'.
4. writeLine—is a Micro-service that writes a given string buffer to 'stdout'. In this Rule, the "writeLine" Micro-service prints a separator line (made of dashes).

The two Micro-services are executed in a loop "foreach" that iterates over the values in the list, which was returned by the acGetIcatResults Micro-service in the variable "*B". For every row in the table returned by acGetIcatResults, both Micro-services are executed.

The listColl.ir Rule prints out the Action value to stdout.

7.1.2 List Checksums for All Files in a Collection

The showicatchksumColl.ir Rule chains one Rule for accessing the list of files and one Micro-service, to obtain the checksum of the file from iCAT, and three other Micro-services to pretty-print the results. The rulegen syntax for this Rule is listed below. This Rule returns an error message if checksums have not been calculated on the files in the collection.

```
myTestRule{
        acGetIcatResults(*Action, *Condition, *B);
        foreach(*B) {
                msiDataObjChksum(*B, *Operation, *C);
                msiGetValByKey(*B, DATA_NAME, *D);
                msiGetValByKey(*B, COLL_NAME, *E);
                writeLine(stdout, "Checksum of *E/*D is *C");
        }
}
INPUT *Action=chksum, *Condition="COLL_NAME = '/tempZone/home/rods/
loopTest'", *Operation=ChksumAll
OUTPUT *Operation, ruleExecOut
```

1. acGetIcatResults—is a Rule that, given an "Action" and an SQL "Condition", returns a table of values. In this case:

"Action": is the "chksum" command
"Condition": COLL_NAME = '/tempZone/home/rods/loopTest'
(this can be any other condition)

2. msiDataObjChksum—is a Micro-service that calculates the checksum for a file and stores it in iCAT when the Operation parameter is set to ChksumAll.
3. msiGetValByKey—is a Micro-service that, given a 'row' in a table and an attribute-name, gets the value for that attribute. It is called twice, first to get the DATA_NAME and then to get COLL_NAME.
4. writeLine—is a Micro-service that can write a given string buffer to 'stdout'. In this Rule, this Micro-service is used to print the checksum of the file in sentence form.

The Micro-Services are executed in a loop "foreach", such that they are executed for every row in the table returned by acGetIcatResults.The Rule prints out the Operation value, as well as the stdout.

7.1.3 Verify Checksum of All Files in a Collection

The verification check done by the Rule verifychksumColl.ir makes sure that the file has not been corrupted since the last checksum was computed (similar to showicatchksumColl.ir).

The Rule chains one Rule for accessing the list of files and one Micro-service to check whether the file's checksum is valid, and three other Micro-services to pretty-print the results. The rulegen syntax for this Rule is:

```
myTestRule{
        acGetIcatResults(*Action, *Condition, *B);
        foreach(*B) {
                msiDataObjChksum(*B, *Operation, *C);
                msiGetValByKey(*B, DATA_NAME, *D);
                msiGetValByKey(*B, COLL_NAME, *E);
                writeLine(stdout, "Checksum of *E/*D is *C");
        }
}
INPUT *Action=chksum, *Condition="COLL_NAME = '/tempZone/home/rods/
loopTest' ", *Operation=verifyChksum
OUTPUT *Operation, ruleExecOut
```

1. acGetIcatResults—A Rule that, given an "Action" and an SQL "Condition", returns a table of values. In this case:

   "Action": chksum
   "Condition": COLL_NAME = '/tempZone/home/rods/loopTest' (this can be any other condition)

2. msiDataObjChksum—A Micro-service that verifies the checksum of the physical file when the Operation parameter is set to verifyChksum.
3. msiGetValByKey—A Micro-service that, given a 'row' in a table and an attribute-name, gets the value for that attribute. It is called twice, first to get DATA_NAME and then to get COLL_NAME.
4. writeLine—A Micro-service that writes a given string buffer to 'stdout'. In this Rule, this Micro-service is used to print the checksum of the file in sentence form.

The Micro-services are executed in a loop "foreach", such that they are executed for every row in the table returned by acGetIcatResults. The Rule prints out the Operation value, as well as the stdout.

7.1.4 Recompute Checksum of All Files in a Collection

The Rule forcechksumColl.ir is used to reset checksums. It recomputes the checksum of all files in a given Collection, and registers them in the iCAT Metadata Catalog (similar to showicatchksum-Coll.ir). The Rule chains one Rule for accessing the list of files and one Micro-service to compute a valid checksum and register it in the iCAT, and three other Micro-services to pretty-print the results. The rulegen syntax for the Rule is:

```
myTestRule{
        acGetIcatResults(*Action, *Condition, *B);
        foreach(*B) {
                msiDataObjChksum(*B, *Operation, *C);
                msiGetValByKey(*B, DATA_NAME, *D);
                msiGetValByKey(*B, COLL_NAME, *E);
                writeLine(stdout, "Checksum of *E/*D is *C");
        }
}
```

```
INPUT *Action=chksum, *Condition="COLL_NAME = '/tempZone/home/rods/
loopTest", *Operation=forceChksum
OUTPUT *Operation, ruleExecOut
```

1. acGetIcatResults—A Rule that, given an a "Action" and an SQL "Condition", returns a table of values. In this case:

   "Action": chksum
   "Condition": COLL_NAME = '/tempZone/home/rods/loopTest' (this can be any other condition)

2. msiDataObjChksum—A Micro-service that computes the checksum of the physical file when the Operation parameter is set to forceChksum.
3. msiGetValByKey—A Micro-service that, given a 'row' in a table and an attribute-name, gets the value for that attribute. It is called twice, first to get DATA_NAME and then to get COLL_NAME.
4. writeLine—A Micro-service that can write a given string buffer to 'stdout'. In this Rule, the Micro-service is used to print the checksum of the file in sentence form.

The Micro-services are executed in a loop "foreach", such that they are executed for every row in the table returned by acGetIcatResults. The Rule prints out the Operation value as well as the stdout. As a side effect, the checksum is computed for each file and registered in the iCAT Metadata Catalog.

7.1.5 Copy Files from Source to Destination Collections

The Rule copyColl.ir makes a copy of each file from a source collection into a destination collection. The new physical copy is stored in a specified storage resource, in this case nvoReplResc. The Rule chains one Rule for accessing the list of files and one Micro-service to make the copy, and other Micro-services to pretty-print the results.

```
myTestRule {
  acGetIcatResults(*Action, *Condition, *B);
   foreach (*B) {
        msiGetValByKey(*B,DATA_NAME,*D);
        msiDataObjCopy(*B, "*DestColl/*D", *Resource, *CC);
        msiGetValByKey(*B,COLL NAME,*E);
```

```
        writeLine(stdout, "Copied *E/*D to *DestColl/*D");
    }
}
INPUT *Action=copy, *Condition="COLL_NAME = '/tempZone/home/rods/
loopTest' ", *Resource=nvoReplResc, *DestColl="/tempZone/home/rods/loopTest2"
OUTPUT *Action, *Condition, *Operation, ruleExecOut
```

1. acGetIcatResults—A Rule that, given an "Action" and an SQL "Condition", returns a table of values. In this case:

"Action":	copy
"Condition":	COLL_NAME = '/tempZone/home/rods/loopTest' (this can be any other condition)

2. msiDataObjCopy—A Micro-service that copies a file from one logical (source) collection to another logical (destination) collection that is physically located in the input *Resource. *CC is the status of the copy operation.
3. msiGetValByKey—A Micro-service that, given a 'row' in a table and an attribute-name, gets the value for that attribute. It is called twice, first to get DATA_NAME and then to get COLL_NAME.
4. writeLine—A Micro-service that can write a given string buffer to 'stdout'. In this Rule, the Micro-service is used to print the location of each original file and the location of the copy of the file.

The Micro-services are executed in a loop "foreach", such that they are executed for every row in the table returned by acGetIcatResults.The Rule prints out the Action, Condition, and Operation values, as well as the stdout. As a side effect, the files are copied into a new collection with separate physical copies.The iCAT Metadata Catalog is modified accordingly.

7.1.6 Make a Replica of Each File in a Collection

The Rule replColl.ir makes a replica of each file in the named collection. The physical replica is stored in a storage resource different from the original file location. The Rule chains one Rule for accessing the list of files and one Micro-service to make the replica, which is executed in a loop (one for each file in the list).

```
myTestRule {
```

```
        acGetIcatResults(*Action, *Condition, *B);
        foreach (*B) {
                msiDataObjRepl(*B, *Resource, *CC);
        }
}
INPUT *Action=replicate, *Condition="COLL_NAME = '/tempZone/home/rods/
loopTest' ", *Resource=$replResc
OUTPUT *Action, *Condition, ruleExecOut
```

1. acGetIcatResults—A Rule that, given an "Action" and an SQL "Condition", returns a table of values. In this case:

   "Action": replicate
   "Condition": COLL_NAME = '/tempZone/home/rods/loopTest'
   (this can be any other condition)

2. msiDataObjRepl—A Micro-service that replicates a file in a Collection (it assigns a different replica number to the new copy in the iCAT Metadata Catalog). Junk contains the status of the operation. In this Rule, the name of the resource is entered interactively. This is accomplished by including a "$" in front of the "*Resource" variable value.

   Executing the irule command will list the default resource as "replResc", and prompt for a new value.

   Default *Resource=replResc
   New *Resource=nvoReplResc

   Entering nvoReplResc will interactively cause the system to use the desired resource.

The Micro-services are executed in a loop "foreach", such that they are executed for every row in the table returned by acGetIcatResults The Rule prints out the Action and Condition values, as well as the stdout. As a side effect, every file is replicated in the same Collection, with a separate physical copy. The iCAT Metadata Catalog is updated accordingly.

7.1.7 Trim the Number of Replicas of a File

The Rule trimColl.ir is used to delete extra replicas of a file. The Rule will do nothing if the number of replicas is less than or equal to a specified number given by 'numCopies'. One can specify which replica is preferable for deletion (by defining a 'replNum') and also specify a given resource whose copy is preferred for deletion. If a resource is specified, only excess copies on that resource, if any, are deleted.

The Rule chains one Rule for accessing the list of files and one Micro-service to trim the number of copies, which is executed in a loop (once for each file in the list).

```
myTestRule {
  acGetIcatResults(*Action, *Condition, *B);
   foreach  (*B)  {
           msiDataObjTrim(*B, *Resource, null, 1, null, *CC);
  }
}
INPUT *Action=trim, *Condition="COLL_NAME = '/tempZone/home/rods/
loopTest' ", *Resource=$replResc
OUTPUT ruleExecOut
```

1. acGetIcatResults—A Rule that, given an "Action" and an SQL "Condition", returns a table of values. In this case:
   "Action": trim
   "Condition": COLL_NAME = '/tempZone/home/rods/loopTest' (this can be any other condition)

2. msiDataObjTrim—A Micro-service that trims extra replicas. The file name is specified by the first parameter. The replica to be deleted is specified by the resource and replNumber parameters. In the example, the preferred resource is given as 'tgReplResc'. The second parameter gives the preferred resource from which to delete the replica. The third parameter in the Micro-service defines the preferred replica to be deleted. In this case, the field is null. The fourth parameter specifies the minimum number of copies to be retained. Here, it is '1', so that at least one copy remains after the trim operation, even if it is a preferred replica number or is located in a preferred resource for deletion. The fifth parameter is useful when performed by an iRODS administrator, and the final parameter is the operation status return.

Note that on execution of this Rule, you will be prompted for the name of the resource to use for the replica. This is caused by the presence of the "$" in front of the *Resource variable value. The Micro-services are executed in a loop "foreach", such that they are executed for every row in the table returned by acGetIcatResults. The Rule prints out only the stdout. As a side effect, the specified file replicas are deleted. The iCAT Metadata Catalog is modified accordingly.

7.2 USER INTERACTION RULES

7.2.1 Send E-Mail to Specified E-Mail Address

The Rule sendMailColl.ir is a variation of showicatchksumColl.ir, which prints out the checksum of all files in a given Collection. In sendMailColl.ir, the results are also sent as an e-mail. The Rule gets a list of files using acGetIcatResults and then calculates the checksum of each file using the msiDataObjChksum Micro-service, and pretty-prints it to stdout using writeLine. The checksum access and pretty-printing are done in a for-loop for each file in the list. After this loop is completed, the sendStdoutAsEmail Micro-service is invoked to send the e-mail.

```
myTestRule{
   acGetIcatResults(*Action, *Condition, *B);
   foreach(*B) {
            msiDataObjChksum(*B, *Operation, *C);
            msiGetValByKey(*B, DATA_NAME, *D);
            msiGetValByKey(*B, COLL_NAME, *E);
            writeLine(stdout, "Checksum of *E/*D is *C");
   }
   sendStdoutAsEmail(*Mailto, "Checksum Results");
}
INPUT *Action=chksum, *Condition="COLL_NAME = '/tempZone/home/rods/
loopTest' ", *Operation=ChksumAll, *Mailto="use-your-email-address"
OUTPUT *Action, *Condition, *Operation, *C, ruleExecOut
```

1. sendStdoutAsEmail—A Micro-service that, given a sendTo parameter (an e-mail address) and a subjectLine parameter, sends out the stdout buffer as the body of the e-mail. In this case, the subject Line is 'Checksum Results'.

The other Micro-services are defined and used as in the showicatchksumColl.ir Rule (see Section 7.1.2, "List Checksums for All Files in a Collection"). The Rule prints out the Action, Condition, Operation, the checksums of the files in the list, and stdout. As a side effect, a single e-mail is sent.

7.2.2 Periodically Verify Checksum of Files

The Rule periodicChksumColl.ir verifies that files have not been corrupted since the last checksum was computed, and sends the results as an e-mail.

The Rule is written as a variation of the verifychksumColl.ir, and sendMailColl.ir Rules; verifychksumColl.ir verifies the checksum of all files in a given Collection and sendMailColl.ir sends the results as an e-mail. The main modification is that the sendMailColl.ir rule-body (with verify instead of show checksum) is executed inside another system Micro-service called delayExec. delayExec queues a given sequence of Micro-services into the queue of the iRODS batch-server, which periodically checks the time and fires the Rule when appropriate. The parameter for delay can be set such that the execution can be done periodically at set intervals.

```
myTestRule{
        delay("<PLUSET>1m</PLUSET><EF>5m</EF>"){
                acGetIcatResults(*Action, *Condition, *B);
                foreach(*B){
                        msiDataObjChksum(*B, *Operation, *C);
                        msiGetValByKey(*B, DATA_NAME, *D);
                        msiGetValByKey(*B, COLL_NAME, *E);
                        writeLine(stdout, "Checksum of *E/*D is *C");
                }
                sendStdoutAsEmail(*Mailto, "Checksum Results");
        }
}
INPUT *Action=chksum, *Condition="COLL_NAME = '/tempZone/home/rods/
loopTest", *Operation=verifyChksum, *Mailto="use-your-email-address"
OUTPUT *Action, *Condition, *Operation, *C, ruleExecOut
```

1. delayExec—is a Micro-service that takes the delayCondition as the first parameter, the Micro-service/rule chain that needs to be executed as the second parameter, and the recovery-Micro-service chain as the third parameter. The delayCondition is given as a tagged condition. In this case, there are two conditions that are specified.

<PLUSET>1m</PLUSET> :	execute the first time after 1 minute has elapsed.
<EF>5m</EF> :	repeat execution every 5 minutes.

The other Micro-services are defined and used as in the verifychksumColl.ir, and sendMailColl.ir Rules.The Rule prints out the Action, Condition, and Operation values, as well as the stdout. As a side effect, an e-mail is sent at specified periodic intervals. To avoid receiving too many messages, execution of this Rule may be turned off by removing the Rule from the queue of outstanding Rules using the iqstat shell command to find the Identifier number of the Rule, and then using the iqdel shell command to delete the Rule.

7.2.3 Remove Expired Files

The Rule purgeCollAndEmail.ir removes files that have expired (current time greater than the time defined by the DATA_EXPIRY parameter in the iCAT Metadata Catalog) and sends the results as an e-mail. The Rule can be easily converted into a periodic Rule. The Rule makes a call to another Rule named acPurgeFiles, which purges all files whose expiration Time is less than the current time, and whose condition matches the given condition. The call also writes to the stdout buffer the names of the files that have been purged. The sendStdoutAsEmail Micro-service call sends the stdout as an e-mail. For the Rule to succeed, the DATA_EXPIRY time will need to be set for each file.

```
myTestRule{
        acPurgeFiles(*Condition);
        sendStdoutAsEmail(*MailTo, "Purge Results");
}
INPUT *Condition="COLL_NAME = '/tempZone/home/rods'/loopTest",
*MailTo="use-your-email-address"
OUTPUT *Condition, ruleExecOut
```

1. acPurgeFiles—A Rule that takes a Condition as a parameter. All files matching that condition and whose expiration time (as given by the iCAT attribute DATA_EXPIRY) is before the current clock time, are deleted. The Rule is very similar to the Rule in copyColl.ir, but makes use of the msiDataObjUnlink Micro-service to perform the deletion and write a message to stdout.
2. sendStdoutAsEmail—A Micro-service that, given a sendTo parameter (an e-mail address) and a subjectLine parameter, sends the stdout buffer as the body of the e-mail. In this case, the subject Line is 'Purge Results'.

The Rule prints out the Condition values as well as the stdout.
As a side effect, files are purged and an e-mail is sent. The iCAT is modified accordingly.

7.3 RULE MANIPULATION

7.3.1 Print Rules Being Used by the Rule Engine

The Rule showCore.ir invokes a Micro-service to pretty-print the Rules being used by the data grid:

```
myTestRule{
        msiAdmShowIRB(*A);
}
INPUT *A=null
OUTPUT ruleExecOut
```

1. msiAdmShowIRB—A Micro-service that reads the data structure in the Rule Engine that holds the current set of Rules, and pretty-prints that structure to the stdout buffer. The Micro-service has a dummy parameter because no input values are actually needed!

No input is necessary. The Rule will display the contents of the current Rule base.

7.3.2 Change the Rules in the Core.Irb File

The Rule chgCoreToCore1.ir pre-pends the Rules in the input file to the Rules in the core.irb file. The input file should be in the server/config/reConfigs directory. The Rule invokes a Micro-service to perform this change. You will need to have administrator privileges to run this Rule. The Rule should be executed on each server to consistently change all of the distributed Rule Bases so that all servers will be running the same policy set. The new Rules will be checked first for execution, before the default Rules in the original core.irb file.

```
myTestRule {
   msiAdmAppendToTopOfCoreIRB(*A);
}
INPUT *A=core.irb.1
OUTPUT *A, ruleExecOut
```

1. msiAdmAppendToTopOfCoreIRB—A Micro-service that pre-pends the given file in the configuration directory 'server/config/reConfigs' onto the core.irb file in the same directory. The next time a new client–server session is started, the newly copied set of Rules will take effect. Note that the core.irb is overwritten. Returning to the original Rule set will require replacing the core.irb file with a copy of the original rules.

The value of *A is printed.

NOTE: The following two Rules:

chgCoreToCore2.ir has *A=core.irb.2

chgCoreToCore3.ir has *A=core.irb.3

and are similar to chgCoreToCore1.ir, except for the input parameter value.

7.3.3 Change Back to the Rules in the Core.Irb.Orig File

The Rule chgCoreToOrig.ir changes the core Rules in the core.irb file in the directory server/config/reConfigs back to that of the core.irb.orig file in the same directory. The Rule invokes a Micro-service to perform this change. You will need to have administrator privileges to run this Rule. The Rule should be executed on each server to consistently change all of the distributed Rule Bases to the same policy set.

```
myTestRule {
   msiAdmChangeCoreIRB(*A);
}
INPUT *A=core.irb.orig
OUTPUT *A, ruleExecOut
```

1. msiAdmChangeCoreIRB—is a Micro-service that copies the specified file in the configuration directory 'server/config/reConfigs' onto the core.irb file in the same directory. The result is that the next time a new client–server session is started, the new set of Rules will take effect. Note that the core.irb is overwritten and all previous content is lost.
   The value of *A is printed.

7.3.4 Pre-Pend Rules

The Rule ruleTest17.ir updates the Rule Base and the Logical Name Mappings for persistent state information and for the functions that implement the Micro-services. From files in the server/config/reConfigs directory, additional Rules are pre-pended to the already existing structures in the Rule Engine. You will need to have administrator privileges to run this Rule. The Rule should be executed on each server to consistently change all of the distributed Rule Bases to the same policy set.

The Rule invokes a Micro-service to perform this addition.

```
myTestRule{
        msiAdmShowIRB(*A);
        msiAdmAddAppRuleStruct(*B,,);
        msiAdmShowIRB(*C);
```

```
}
INPUT *B="core2"
OUTPUT *B, ruleExecOut
```

1. msiAdmAddAppRuleStruct—A Micro-service that reads the given file in the configuration directory 'server/config/reConfigs' and pre-pends them to the Rule list being used by the Rule Engine. These Rules are loaded at the beginning of the core.irb file, and because they are checked to run first can thus be used to override the core Rules from the core.irb file.

   This Micro-service can also be used to pre-pend a new Micro-service name mapping file (*.fnm, defined in the second argument) and a new variable name mapping file (*.dvm, defined in the third argument) to the top of the mapping, thus effectively overriding the original definitions. The changes made are not permanent. They exist until another change at the end of the client–server session. In contrast, the chgCoreToCore1.ir Micro-service changes the content of the core.irb file, and hence is permanent and is loaded when all future client–server sessions are started.

In this Rule, the core file name is 'core2' (the .irb extension is not needed), which is given as the first parameter of the msiAdmAddAppRuleStruct Micro-service. Only the core.irb file is updated. The other two parameters of the Micro-service are left as null strings in this case. The Micro-service msiAdmShowIRB is used to show the content of the Rule structure. Remember that msiAdmShowIRB uses a dummy argument. Hence, *A and *C do not need to be set.

The Rules in the core.irb file are printed before and after the update.

7.3.5 Pre-Pend Rules and Logical Name Mappings

The Rule ruleTest18.ir pre-pends (not changes!) Rules, function map names, and variable map names from files in the server/config/reConfigs directory to the already existing structures in the Rule Engine. See Section 7.3.4 ("Pre-Pend Rules") for more information on the msiAdmAdd AppRuleStruct Micro-service that is used. You will need to have administrator privileges to run this Rule. The Rule should be executed on each server to consistently change all of the distributed Rule Bases to the same policy set.

This Rule invokes one Micro-service to perform the addition and another to print the Session Variable data-value-mapping, before and after the addition. The data-value-mapping is used to provide logical names to the values in the whiteboard (REI structure). For example, when one uses the variable "userNameClient" (e.g., in ruleTest16.ir), it points to a particular value in the complex REI structure: rei→uoic→userName.

```
myTestRule {
   msiAdmShowDVM(*A);
   msiAdmAddAppRuleStruct(*B,*B,*B);
  msiAdmShowDVM(*C);
}

INPUT *B=core2
OUTPUT *B, ruleExecOut
```

1. msiAdmShowDVM is a Micro-service that reads the data-value-mapping data structure in the Rule Engine and pretty-prints that structure to the stdout buffer. The Micro-service uses a dummy parameter!

In this Rule, all three structures—Rules, data-value-mappings, and function-name mappings—are changed.The values of *B and stdout are printed. The files that are added are core2.irb (Rules), core2.dvm (Session Variable name mappings), and core2.fnm (micro-service name mappings).

7.3.6 Append Rules and Logical Name Mappings

The Rule ruleTest19.ir appends (not changes!) the Rules, function map names, and variable map names from files in the server/config/reConfigs directory to the already existing structures in the Rule Engine. See ruleTest17.ir for more information on the msiAdmAddAppRuleStruct Micro-service that is used. You will need to have administrator privileges to run this Rule. The Rule should be executed on each server to consistently change all of the distributed Rule Bases to the same policy set.

The Rule invokes a Micro-service to perform this addition and another to print the function-name-mapping before and after the addition. The function-name-mapping is used to map from logical names of Micro-services to internal function names that are compiled in the server code. For example, in core.fnm there is a mapping from the name openObj to the name msiDataObjOpen. Hence, if one writes a Rule using openObj (using the same parametric sequence), then internally the C function msiDataObjOpen would be invoked. This way one can use a logical name for a Micro-service and lazily map it at run time to a physical function name. The msiAdmAddAppRuleStruct provides a means for doing this on the fly.

```
myTestRule {
   msiAdmShowFNM(*A);
```

```
    msiAdmAddAppRuleStruct(*B,*B,*B);
  msiAdmShowFNM(*C);
  }
  INPUT *B=core2
  OUTPUT *B, ruleExecOut
```

1. msiAdmShowFNM is a Micro-service that reads the function-name-mapping data structure in the Rule Engine and pretty-prints that structure to the stdout buffer. The Micro-service has a dummy parameter!

In this Rule, all three structures—Rules, data-value-mappings, and function-name mappings—are changed using the files core2.irb, core2.dvm, and core2.fnm. The values of *B and stdout are printed. The entries in the FNM structure are printed before and after the update.

7.3.7 Replicate Each File in a Collection

The Rule replCollDelayed.ir makes a replica of each file in a Collection, but at a later time. The body of the Rule is quite different from that of replColl.ir, which uses a forEachExec Micro-service to create individual file replicas. In this case, a new Micro-service is used to perform Collection-level replication.

```
myTestRule {
   delayExec(<PLUSET>1m</PLUSET>) {
         msiReplColl(*desc_coll,*desc_resc, "backupMode", *outbuf);
   }
}
INPUT *desc_coll="/tempZone/home/rods/repl_test"
OUTPUT *desc_resc=demoResc2
```

1. msiReplColl—is a Micro-service that replicates a Collection (giving a different replica number to each newly replicated file) into a new directory specified by the first argument. In this case, the replica is physically stored in the 'demoResc2' Resource, which is given as the second parameter of the Micro-service. The third parameter is a string that provides information about the type of replication being made; the value for this parameter can be an empty string, in which case all files are replicated, or it can be 'backupMode' in which case, if a good copy already exists in the destination resource, the Rule will not perform a replication. The fourth parameter outputs the status of the operation.

The Micro-service is executed in a delayExec mode with a 1-minute delay. See Section 7.2.2 ("Periodically Verify Checksum Of Files"), which describes the periodicChksumCollColl.ir Rule for more information on the delayExec Micro-service. The Rule prints out the stdout. As a side effect, the files are replicated in the same Collection with separate physical copies. The iCAT is modified accordingly.

7.4 SYSTEM TESTING

7.4.1 Test Parametric Variable

Three versions of a Rule exist for testing manipulation of parametric variables. The versions are labeled ruleTest1.ir, ruleTest2.ir, and ruleTest3.ir. The Rule ruleTest1.ir assigns the result of evaluating a conditional expression to a parametric variable (*-variable). The conditional expression in this Rule checks whether the iRODS client user name is equivalent to the string expression r*s (* is a wild card string character). So, for example, if the user is rods, it will evaluate to 1. If there is no string expression match, then 0 is assigned.

```
myTestRule{
        assign(*A, "$userNameClient like r*s");
}
INPUT *A = null
OUTPUT *A
```

1. **Assign**—A system Micro-service. The value of the second parameter is assigned to the first parameter, after an evaluation is performed, if needed.

The assign Micro-service can also be used to evaluate arithmetic operations:

```
myTestRule3{
        assign(*A, 200 + 300);
}
INPUT *A=null
OUTPUT *A
```

1. **Assign**—A system Micro-service. The value of the second parameter is assigned to the first parameter, after the operations are performed, if needed.

Note that white space around the operations is critical. The "+" symbol needs both a preceding space and a following space for the addition to be performed. If the spaces are not present, the value of A will be the string "200 + 300" instead of the numeric value "500". The value of A is printed provided the Rule is executed with the –v option:

```
irule –vF ruleTest1.ir
```

The operation in this Rule is a simple addition.The Rule prints out the value of *A.

7.4.2 Test $-Variable

Four versions of Rules for testing Session Variables are available: ruleTest4.ir, ruleTest5.ir, ruleTest6.ir, and ruleTest7.ir. They assign values to a Whiteboard Variable (REI variable), or a session $-variable.

ruleTest4.ir: test assignment to string session $-variables, also known as whiteboard (REI) variables.

```
myTestRule {
        assign(*A,$rodsZoneClient);
        assign($rodsZoneClient,$userNameClient);
        assign(*B,$rodsZoneClient);
    }
  INPUT *D=200 + 200
  OUTPUT *A, *B, *D
```

1. Assign—A system Micro-service. The value of the second parameter is assigned to the first parameter, after any evaluation is performed, if needed.

This Rule first assigns *A to the value of $rodsZoneClient (client's Zone name), then assigns $rodsZoneClient to $userNameClient (client's user name), and lastly assigns *B to the current value in $rodsZoneClient. The test will be correct if *A prints the client's zone name, and *B prints the client's user name. D will be a string that contains "200 + 200".

ruleTest5.ir: test assignment to numeric $–variables.

```
myTestRule {
      assign(*A,$sysUidClient);
        assign(*C, 200 + 300 );
```

```
        assign($sysUidClient, 200 + 300 );
        assign(*B,$sysUidClient) ;
}
    INPUT *A=null
    OUTPUT *A, *B, *C
```

This Rule first assigns *A to the value of $sysUidClient(client's iRODS identifier), then assigns the sum of 200+300 to $sysUidClient, and lastly assigns *B to the current value in $sysUidClient. The test will be correct if *A is 0, and *C and *B are 500.

ruleTest6.ir: test assignment to numeric $-variables.

This Rule is the same as ruleTest5.ir, but takes the values of assignment from a parametric variable instead of a string.

```
myTestRule {
        assign(*A,$sysUidClient);
        assign(*C, *D );
assign($sysUidClient, *D );
        assign(*B,$sysUidClient);
}
INPUT *D=200 + 200
OUTPUT *A, *B, *C, *D
```

Note that *D is a string, but when it is evaluated within the assign statement, it is converted to a sum. The Rule works correctly when A is 0, C is 400, and B is 400.

ruleTest7.ir: test assignment to both parametric and whiteboard Session Variables.

```
mytestRule {
    assign(*A,$userNameClient);
    assign(*B,$userNameProxy);
    assign($userNameClient,alpha);
    assign(*C,$userNameClient);
    assign($userClient,$userProxy);
    assign(*D,$userNameClient);
    assign(*F,$userNameProxy);
    }
```

```
INPUT *D=200 + 200
OUTPUT *A, *B, *C, *D, *E
```

The Rule works if the values of A, B, D, and E are your user name, and the value of C is "alpha".

7.4.3 Test "While" Loop Execution

The Rule ruleTest8.ir initializes a value for a while loop variable (*A), and then executes a while Micro-service.

```
myTestRule {
        assign(*A, 0);
        while (*A < 20) {
                assign(*A, "*A + 4");
                writeLine(stdout, "A = *A");
        }
}
INPUT *A=4
OUTPUT *A, ruleExecOut
```

1. whileExec—A Micro-service that executes a while loop. The first argument is a condition that will be checked on each loop iteration. The second argument is the body of the while loop, given as a sequence of Micro-services, and the third argument is the recoveryBody for recovery from failures.

Note that the input value of *A is overwritten by the first assign statement in the Rule. An initial assignment of 0 is made to the loop variable *A and is incremented by 4 every time the loop is executed. In this example, the loop terminates when *A is greater than or equal to 20. The Rule will print out five lines with "A = 4", "A = 8", "A = 12", "A = 16", and "A = 20".

No input is needed, even though some are given in this example.

7.4.4 Test "For" Loop Execution

The Rule ruleTest9.ir executes a "for loop" using the forExec Micro-service and prints a sequence.

```
myTestRule{
    for (*A = 0; *A < *D; *A = *A + 4) {
```

```
                writeLine(stdout, *A);
        }
}
INPUT *A=1000, *D= "(199 * 2) + 200"
OUTPUT *A, *D, ruleExecOut
```

1. forExec—A Micro-service that executes a for loop. The first argument is an assignment to a loop-variable. The second argument is a condition check before executing the "for loop", and the third argument is an assignment statement that increments (or decrements) the loop variable. The loop variable can be a string with string conditional checking. The fourth argument is the body of the "for loop", given as a sequence of Micro-services, and the fifth argument is the recoveryBody for recovery from failures.

Within the Rule, the initial assignment of 0 is made to the loop variable *A and is incremented by 4 every time the loop is executed. The loop prints to stdout the value of *A, followed by a line break. The loop terminates when *A is greater than or equal to *D, which is an input parameter set to (199 * 2) + 200.

The Rule executes correctly if the value of stdout prints a sequence 0, 4, 8, 12, …, 596, each number in a separate line. Note that quotes are needed on the *D input string, and that spaces are required before and after the "*" and the "+" operators.

7.4.5 Test "If-Then-Else" Execution

The Rule ruleTest10.ir executes an "if-then-else" conditional test using the ifExec Micro-service.

```
myTestRule{
        if (*A < *D) then
                *A = *D;
        else
                *D = *A;
}
INPUT *A = "$1000", *D = "$ (199 * 2) + 200"
OUTPUT *A, *D
```

1. ifExec—A Micro-service that executes an if-then-else statement. The ifExec Micro-service has six arguments. The first argument is a conditional check. If the check is successful (TRUE), the Micro-service sequence in the second argument will be executed. If the

check fails, then the Micro-service sequence in the fourth argument will be executed. The third argument is the recoveryBody for recovery from failures for the then-part, and the sixth argument is the recoveryBody for recovery from failures for the else-part.

The Rule prompts for new values for both *A and *D. The Rule works correctly if it prints out values for *A and *D of 1000.

7.4.6 Test Writing to Stdout and Stderr Buffers

The Rules ruleTest11.ir and ruleTest12.ir execute a writeString Micro-service. In the white board (REI structure), there is a structure called ruleExecOut that is part of the msParamArray for emulating writing to stdout and stderr buffers. These buffers are part of REI and are not actually written to the screen or console immediately. This structure provides a means to buffer output string messages from the Micro-services. When irule completes execution of the Rule, the buffers can be printed out to the screen. This printing is accomplished by adding ruleExecOut as an output argument to the ruleTest11.ir file. The ruleExecOut structure is passed along for every Micro-service execution (including remote and delayed executions), and hence can provide serial capture of messages across multiple Micro-service invocations.

ruleTest11.ir: Write strings to stdout and stderr. No end-of-line is inserted at the end of a string. This will concatenate the output lines within the buffer.

```
myTestRule {
    writeString(stdout,"alpha beta gamma");
    writeString(stdout,"alpha beta gamma");
    writeString(stderr,"Error:blah");
  }
  INPUT *A=null
  OUTPUT ruleExecOut
```

1. writeString—A Micro-service that writes to a stderr or stdout buffer in the ruleExecOut structure. The first argument is the buffer name (stderr and stdout are the two buffers currently supported). The second argument is the string to be written to the buffer.

The Rule writes the same string twice to stdout and another string to stderr. A successful execution will show

```
strerr = Error:blah        stdout = alpha beta gammaalpha beta gamma
```

These will be printed out to screen.

ruleTest12.ir: Writes lines to stdout and stderr. An end-of-line is inserted after each write.

```
myTestRule {
    writeLine(stdout,"alpha beta gamma");
    writeLine(stdout,"alpha beta gamma");
    writeLine(stderr,"Error:blah");
  }
  INPUT *A=null
  OUTPUT ruleExecOut
```

The Rule writes the same string twice to stdout and another string to stderr. A successful execution will print out each on a separate line. These will be printed out to the screen.

7.4.7 Test Sending E-Mail

The Rule ruleTest13.ir executes the msiSendMail Micro-service to send e-mail.

```
myTestRule {
        msiSendMail("your-email-address","irods test","mail sent by an msi.did you get
this");
}
INPUT *A=null
OUTPUT ruleExecOut
```

1. msiSendMail—A Micro-service that sends e-mail using the mail command in the Unix system. The first argument is the e-mail address of the receiver. The second argument is the subject string and the third argument is the body of the e-mail. No attachments are supported. The sender of the e-mail is the Unix usr-id running the irodsServer.

The side effect of the Rule is that an e-mail is sent to the specified recipient.

7.4.8 Test "For Each" Loop for Comma-Separated List

The Rule ruleTest14.ir executes a loop using the forEachExec Micro-service, based on a list of items given to the Micro-service.

```
myTestRule {
        foreach ( *A ) {
              writeLine(stdout,*A);
        }
}
INPUT *A= "123,345,567,aa,bb,678"
OUTPUT ruleExecOut
```

1. forEachExec—A Micro-service that executes a loop for every item in a list given as the first argument. The list can be a comma-separated string (STR_MS_T), array of strings (StrArray_MS_T), array of integers (IntArray_MS_T), or iCAT query result (GenQuery-Out_MS_T). The second argument is the body of the foreach loop, given as a sequence of Micro-services, and the third argument is the recoveryBody for recovery from failures.

The Rule takes a comma-separated string and prints every item in that list through the stdout.

7.4.9 Test "For Each" Loop on a Query Result

Rule ruleTest15.ir executes a loop using the forEachExec Micro-service to process a table of rows. The table is generated by a query on the iCAT metadata catalog.

```
myTestRule {
msiExecStrCondQuery(*A '%rods%', *B);
        foreach ( *B ) {
              msiPrintKeyValPair(stdout,*B);
              writeLine(stdout,*K);
        }
}
INPUT A= "SELECT DATA_NAME, DATA_REPL_NUM, DATA_CHECKSUM
 WHERE DATA_NAME LIKE", *K= "---------------------- "
OUTPUT ruleExecOut
```

1. forEachExec—A Micro-service that executes a loop for very item in a list given as the first argument. The list can be a comma-separated string (STR_MS_T), array of strings (StrArray_MS_T), array of integers (IntArray_MS_T), or iCAT query result (GenQuery Out_MS_T). The second argument is the body of the foreach loop, given as a sequence of Micro-services, and the third argument is the recoveryBody for recovery from failures.

2. msiExecStrCondQuery—A Micro-service that, given an iCAT query, executes it and returns the list in a tabular row structure (GenQueryOut_MS_T).
3. msiPrintKeyValPair—A Micro-service that takes a row-structure from GenQueryOut_MS_T and prints it as a ColumnName=Value pair.

The Rule uses the result (tabular) from execution of an iCAT query. The Micro-service msiExecStrCondQuery is used to run the query:

SELECT DATA_NAME, DATA_REPL_NUM, DATA_CHECKSUM WHERE DATA_NAME LIKE '%rods%'.

Each file that contains the string "rods" within the name is added to the result list. The result is printed using the msiPrintKeyValPair Micro-service, which prints each row as an attribute–value pair. A separator line is printed after each row.The Rule prints out the query and the stdout.

ruleTest16.ir: Loop over a result list generated by using the acGetIcatResults Micro-service.

```
myTestRule {
acGetIcatResults(*Action,*Condition,*B);
        foreach ( *B ) {
            msiPrintKeyValPair(stdout,*B);
            writeLine(stdout,*K) ;
        }
}
INPUT *Action=list, *Condition= "COLL_NAME = '/tempZone/home/rods' ", *K= "--
----------- "
OUTPUT ruleExecOut
```

The Rule will list all of the files in the chosen collection, along with information about the DATA_RESC_NAME, DATA_REPL_NUM, and DATA_SIZE.

7.4.10 Test Remote Execution of Micro-Service Writes

The Rule ruleTest20.ir invokes the remoteExec Micro-service to execute remotely a given sequence of Micro-services.

```
myTestRule {
    writeLine(stdout,begin);
    writeLine(stdout, "just write in srbbrick1 ");
    remoteExec(andal.sdsc.edu,null) {
        writeLine(stdout, "remote write in andal ");
    }
    remoteExec(andal.sdsc.edu,null) {
        writeLine(stdout, "remote write again in andal ");
    }
    remoteExec(srbbrick14.sdsc.edu,null) {
        writeLine(stdout, "remote write in srbbrick1 ");
    }
    remoteExec(andal.sdsc.edu,null) {
        writeLine(stdout, "remote write again and again in andal ");
    }
    remoteExec(srbbrick14.sdsc.edu,null) {
        writeLine(stdout, "again remote write in srbbrick1 ");
    }
    remoteExec(andal.sdsc.edu,null) {
        writeLine(stdout, "remote write third in andal ");
    }
    remoteExec(srbbrick14.sdsc.edu,null) {
        writeLine(stdout, "second remote write in srbbrick1 ");
    }
    remoteExec(srbbrick14.sdsc.edu,null) {
        writeLine(stdout, "third remote write in srbbrick1 ");
    }
    writeLine(stdout, "again just write in srbbrick1 ");
    writeLine(stdout, "end ");
}
INPUT A*=null
OUTPUT ruleExecOut
```

1. remoteExec—A Micro-service that remotely executes a Micro-service chain on another iRODS Server. The first argument is the remote server's network id; the second argument

is the sequence of Micro-services to be remotely executed; and the third argument is the recoveryBody for recovery from failures.

In this Rule, the original Rule is invoked on srbbrick14.sdsc.edu, which in turn calls remote executions at another server (andal.sdsc.edu) and remote calls to itself. No input is used, and the stdout is printed.

7.4.11 Test Remote Execution of Delayed Writes

The Rule ruleTest21.ir invokes the remoteExec Micro-service to execute a given sequence of Micro-services remotely that are delayed 10 seconds before execution.

```
myTestRule {
 writeLine(stdout,"begin");
 remoteExec(andal.sdsc.edu,null) {
  msiSleep(10,0);
  writeLine(stdout,"open remote write in andal");
  remoteExec(srbbrick14.sdsc.edu,null) {
   msiSleep(10,0);
   writeLine(stdout, "remote of a remote write in srbbrick1");
  }
remoteExec(srbbrick14.sdsc.edu,null) {
 remoteExec(andal.sdsc.edu,null) {
  msiSleep(10,0);
  writeLine(stdout, "remote of a remote of a remote write in andal");
  }
 }
 msiSleep(10,0);
 writeLine(stdout, "close remote write in andal");
 }
 writeLine(stdout, "end") ;
}
INPUT *A=null
OUTPUT ruleExecOut
```

1. remoteExec—A Micro-service that remotely executes a Micro-service chain on another iRODS Server. The first argument is the remote server's network i.d., the second argument

is the sequence of Micro-services to be remotely executed, and the third argument is the recoveryBody for recovery from failures.

In this Rule, the original execution is invoked on srbbrick14.sdsc.edu and a line is printed to that effect; then, a remote execution is invoked on a server called andal.sdsc.edu, which after sleeping for 10 seconds and writing a message, calls a remote execution back on srbbrick14.sdsc.edu, which, after sleeping for 10 seconds and writing a message, returns back to andal.sdsc.edu. At andal.sdsc.edu the execution again calls for a remote execution at srbbrick14.sdsc.edu, which immediately executes a remote execution at andal.sdsc.edu, which sleeps and writes a message. Control then reverts back to srbbrick14.sdsc.edu, which in turn gives it to andal.sdsc.edu, which sleeps and writes one more message before returning back to the original invocation at srbbrick14.sdsc.edu, which prints an end message. No input is used. The stdout is printed.

7.5 RESOURCE SELECTION EXAMPLE

In the server/config/reConfigs/core.irb file there is a Rule (number 1016) called "acSetRescSchemeForCreate", which is used for setting the resource preferences. By default, this Rule is (in iRODS Rule syntax):

```
acSetRescSchemeForCreate||msiSetDefaultResc(demoResc,null)|nop
```

which basically sets 'demoResc' as a default resource if no resource is specified.

This Rule can be modified to randomly select a storage resource from a group of resources as follows:

```
acSetRescSchemeForCreate||msiSetDefaultResc(demoResc,null)##
msiSetRescSortScheme(random)
                    |nop##nop
(all of above in one line—no line breaks)
```

Adding the "msiSetRescSortScheme" to the Rule executes a random pick of one of the resources. If you want to force everyone to use your resource, you can change the first Micro-service in the Rule to:

```
msiSetDefaultResc(my_group,forced)
```

This will override the resource given by the client.

An additional feature of this Micro-service is that if you do not like the random sorting method used in the default Micro-service, you can write your own and use that in the "acSetRescSchemeForCreate" Rule and achieve your goal.

As you can see, there are no conditions being checked; "||" is used in the above Rule for the condition. You can add Rules to the core.irb file with different conditions (you need at least one catchall Rule as the default Rule in case no conditions are satisfied), which can use different resource sets and different selection criteria as you prefer, with conditions determined on a collection basis or a user/group basis, or both.

This level of customization provides in-depth control of resource management, which can make life easier or harder for the data manager.

• • • •

CHAPTER 8

Extending iRODS

In addition to the large number of generic features, the iRODS Data Grid is highly extensible to support specific applications. New Micro-services can be added, new Rules can be created, and new state information can be saved in the iCAT. This means the iRODS Data Grid can evolve. A new collection can be created that is governed by the new Rules and Micro-services and the associated state information. The new collection can be run in parallel with an original collection, which is still governed by the original Rules, Micro-services, and state information. The user of the data grid can then migrate files from the collection managed by the old policies to the collection managed by the new policies. Detailed instructions are available on how to apply these extensions to an iRODS Data Grid.

8.1 CHANGING THE IP ADDRESS

The iRODS Data Grid assumes that a fixed IP address is used for the iRODS Servers and the iCAT metadata catalog. If a system is moved to a new IP address, multiple parameters need to be reset to enable communication to be established between the servers.

Upon installation, it is possible to have the system use LOCALHOST for the IP address. This makes it possible to set up systems that are self-contained, and suitable for giving demonstrations. The use of LOCALHOST can be set up during installation by setting the Environment Variable USE_LOCALHOST before running irodssetup. For example, if you are using the bash shell, you would type:

```
USE_LOCALHOST=1
export USE_LOCALHOST
```

Another way to accomplish this is to disconnect from the network before installing the software. The installation procedure will automatically use LOCALHOST for the IP address.

To modify the IP address of an existing installation, use the following steps:

- Stop iRODS and PostgreSQL:
  irodsctl stop

- Edit each of the following files, changing the host name to the new address:
  - .odbc.ini in the home directory
  - .irods/.irodsEnv in home directory
  - pgsql/etc/odbc.ini in the Postgres directory
  - server/config/server.config in iRODS distribution directory
- Then start iRODS again:
  - irodsctl start
- And modify the address of the local resource:
  - iadmin modresc demoResc host *new-host-name*

8.2 HOW TO INTERFACE A MICRO-SERVICE

Micro-services can be added as either system Micro-services in the server area, or as Module Micro-services that are compiled only as necessary for a given application. We discuss both options below.

8.2.1 How to Interface a Micro-Service as a Module

This requires a two-step process:

1. Create a Module, which is done once for each Module.
2. Add a Micro-service to the Module, which is done for every new Micro-service that is added to the Module.

Creating a module. A "Module" is a bundle of optional software components for iRODS. Typically, a Module provides specialized Micro-services. Modules also may provide new Rules, library functions, commands, and even application servers. Once you have developed the software to perform a new iRODS function, you can add your software as a new iRODS Module through the following steps:

1. Create a directory named for the Module:
   - mkdir modules/*MODNAME*
2. Move into that directory:
   - cd modules/*MODNAME*
3. Create one or more subdirectories for the components being added to iRODS:
   - mkdir microservices
   - mkdir rules
   - mkdir lib

```
mkdir clients
mkdir servers
```

For the rest of these instructions, we will assume you are adding Micro-services, but similar instructions apply for other additions.

4. Create source, include, and object subdirectories:

```
mkdir microservices/src
mkdir microservices/include
mkdir microservices/obj
```

5. Add source and include files to the "src" and "include" directories.
6. Create a Makefile by copying one from an existing Module, such as "properties":

```
cp ../properties/Makefile.
```

7. Edit the Makefile to list your source files and add any special compile flags or libraries you may need. The Makefile must respond to a set of standard targets:

all	build everything
microservices	build new microservices
client	build new clients
server	build new servers
rules	build new rules
clean	remove built objects, etc.
client_cflags	compile flags for building clients
client_ldflags	link flags for building clients
server_cflags	compile flags for building servers
server_ldflags	link flags for building servers

The Micro-services, client, and server targets should compile your code. The client and server targets should link your custom clients and servers. If your Module does not have one or more of these, the target should exist but do nothing.

The client and server flag targets should echo to stdout the compiler or linker flags needed on *other* clients and servers that use the Module. The "cflags" echos should list -I include paths and specific include files. The "ldflags" echos should list -L link paths, -l library names, and specific library or object files.

8. Create an info.txt file by copying one from an existing Module:

```
cp ../properties/info.txt.
```

9. Edit the info.txt file to include information about your Module. The file must contain:

Name:	the name of the Module
Brief:	a short description of the Module
Description:	a longer description of the Module

Dependencies:	a list of Modules this Module needs
Enabled:	whether the Module is enabled by default

Each of these must be on a single (possibly long) line. For dependencies, list Module names separated by white space. Module names must match exactly the directory name of other Modules. Case matters.

How to use a module's info.txt. The "info.txt" file in a Module's top-level directory describes the Module. It is intended for use by the iRODS Makefile and configuration scripts.

The file is a list of keyword–value pairs, one per line. For instance:

Name:	sample
Brief:	A sample microservice Module
Description:	This is a sample Module description.
Dependencies:	example
Enabled:	yes
Creator:	University of California, San Diego
Created:	Sept 2007
License:	BSD

Name: The name of the Module. The name should match the Module directory name.

Brief: A brief half-line description of the Module. The iRODS configure script uses this value when printing help information about available Modules.

Description: A longer description of the Module. Although the value must be on a single line, it can be several sentences long.

Dependencies: A list of Module names upon which the Module depends. Names should be space-separated and must match Module directory names. The iRODS configure script uses this to ensure that all Modules that must be enabled together are enabled together.

Enabled: The value "yes" or "no" indicates whether the Module should be enabled by default. The iRODS configure script uses this to set defaults on configuring iRODS.

Creator: The name of the principal individual or organization responsible for creating the Module.

Created: The approximate creation date of the Module.

License: The license covering the Module's source code. Additional information may be in the source files or in Module documentation. This value is only used as a general indicator.

A Doxygen application processes the source code, extracting text fields for documentation. A default Doxygen script processes comments that are inserted in each Micro-service.

Adding a micro-service to a module. All Micro-service functions are discovered by the iRODS Server by reading a master "action" table compiled into the Server. The action table is split into three files:

1. server/re/include/reAction.header
2. server/re/include/reAction.table
3. server/re/include/reAction.footer

The iRODS Makefiles assemble these files and those provided by Modules to build the file server/re/include/reAction.h. This file contains:

- reAction.header —The header for each Micro-service Module.
- reAction.table —The table entries for each Micro-service Module.
- reAction.footer

There are two ways to add a Micro-service:

(1) For system Micro-services
  - Edit reAction.header to add function prototypes
  - Edit reAction.table to add table initializations

(2) For Module Micro-services
  1. Create MODNAME/microservices/include/microservices.header. Edit this to add function prototypes.
  2. Create MODNAME/microservices/include/microservices.table. Edit this to add table initializations.

Function prototypes declare the C Micro-service function. Although these can be added to the above files directly, authors are encouraged to use a separate include file and just add a #include of that file. For instance, here is a typical Micro-services.header file for a Module:

```
// Sample module microservices
#include "sampleMS.h"
```

The reAction.table and each Module's microservices.table file contains a C array initialization listing all available Micro-services. Each line in the initialization looks like this:

```
// Sample module microservices
{ "sample", 2, (funcPtr) msiSample },
```

There are three values, in order:

1. The service name is the user-visible name of the Micro-service. It is a string using letters, numbers, and underbars. It should be descriptive and need not match the Micro-service function name.
2. The argument count is the number of msParam_t arguments for the function. It does not include the ruleExecInfo_t argument.
3. The function name is a pointer to the C function for the Micro-service.

How to rebuild reAction.h. The server's reAction.h action table is automatically rebuilt by the iRODS root Makefile if any include file changes in server/re/include or modules/*/microservices/include. To force reAction.h to be rebuilt, delete the existing file and run the "reaction" Makefile target:

```
rm server/re/include/reAction.h
make reaction
```

How to interface a system (server) micro-service

1. Create the Micro-service function as needed.

```
int myPetProc(char *in1, int in2, char *out1, int *out2)
{
  ... my favorite code ...
}
```

2. Create the Micro-service interface (msi) glue procedure.

```
int msiMyPetProc(msParam_t *mPin1, msParam_t *mPin2,
            msParam_t *mPout1, msParam_t *mPout2,
            RuleExecInfo_t *rei)
{
 char *in1,  out1;
 int i, in2, out2;

 RE_TEST_MACRO ("    Calling myPetProc")
 /* the above line is needed for loop back testing using the irule -i option */

 in1  = (char *) mPin1->inOutStruct;
 in2  = (int)    mPin2->inOutStruct;
 out1 = (char *) mPout1->inOutStruct;
 out2 = (int)    mPout2->inOutStruct;

 i = myPetProc(in1, in2, out1, &out2);
 mPout2->inOutStruct = (int) out2;

 return(i);
}
```

3. Define the msi call in the file server/re/include/reAction.table by adding the function signature in the area where all function signatures are defined.

   ```
   int msiMyPetProc(msParam_t *mPin1, msParam_t *mPin2, msParam_t *mPout1,
   msParam_t *mPout2, RuleExecInfo_t *rei);
   ```

4. Register the Micro-service by making an entry in the file server/re/include/reAction.table. The first item in the entry is the external name of the Micro-service, the second is the number of user-defined arguments for the msi procedure call (excluding the RuleExecInfo_t *rei), and the third argument is the name of the msi procedure. Note that the names are the same in the following example for the first and third values in the entry. We recommend this format for clarity purposes:

   ```
   {"msiMyPetProc", 4, (funcPtr) msiMyPetProc}
   ```

5. If there are any 'include' files that are needed, they can be added to server/re/include/reAction.header.
6. Define the called procedure in an appropriate include file (for the present reFuncDefs.h file would be a reasonable place for this, since this will require no change in any Makefile) by adding the signature.

```
int myPetProc(char *in1, int in2, char *out1, int *out2);
```

The Micro-service is now ready for compilation and use!

8.3 WEB SERVICES AS MICRO-SERVICES

Web services can be turned into Micro-services. The iRODS Data Grid already has some Micro-services that invoke Web services as part of the release. Interfacing a Web service is a slightly involved process. There are two steps for encapsulating web services in Micro-services.

1. The first step is to build a common library that can be used by all Micro-services that connect to web services. This is done ONLY ONCE.
2. The second step is done for each Micro-service that is built.

8.3.1 First Step (Done Only Once)

1. Acquire the gsoap distribution. This can be found at: http://sourceforge.net/projects/gsoap2 or other mirrored sites.
2. Put the files in the webservices/gsoap directory.
3. Build the gsoap libraries and copy them to appropriate directories (See README.txt in the gsoap distribution for more information on building.)

```
cd gsoap
./configure
./make
cd soapcpp2
cp libgsoap++.a  libgsoap.a  libgsoapck++.a libgsoapck.a  libgsoapssl++.a libgsoapssl.a
../../microservices/lib
cp stdsoap2.h ../../microservices/include
cp stdsoap2.c stdsoap2.h ../../microservices/src/common
cd ../../microservices/src/common
```

```
rm *
touch env.h
../../../gsoap/soapcpp2/src/soapcpp2 -c -penv env.h
gcc -c -DWITH_NONAMESPACES envC.c
gcc -c -DWITH_NONAMESPACES stdsoap2.c
cp envC.o stdsoap2.o ../../obj
```

4. Add a file called info.txt in the webservices directory if it is not already there. The content of this file is similar to that of the info.txt file in the modules/properties directory.
5. Make sure that the value for "Enabled" in the info.txt file is "yes" (instead of "no").
6. Add the word 'webservices' (without the quotes) to the MODULES option in the ~/iRODS/config/mk/config file. Make sure that the line is not commented out

```
MODULES- webservices properties
```

8.3.2 Second Step (Done for Each Web Service)

Here, we show an example Micro-service being built for getting a stockQuotation. Building a Micro-service for a web service is a multistep process. If not already enabled, enable the Micro-services for web services by changing the enabling flag to 'yes' in the file modules/webservices/info.txt

1. mkdir webservices/microservices/src/stockQuote
2. Place stockQuote.wsdl in the directory webservices/microservices/src/stockQuote. The wsdl file is obtained from the web services site.
3. cd webservices/microservices/src/stockQuote
4. setenv GSOAPDIR ../../../gsoap/soapcpp2
5. $GSOAPDIR/wsdl/wsdl2h -c -I$GSOAPDIR -o stockQuoteMS_wsdl.h stockQuote.wsdl

   This creates a file called stockQuoteMS_wsdl.h

6. $GSOAPDIR/src/soapcpp2 -c -w -x -C -n -pstockQuote stockQuoteMS_wsdl.h

   This creates files: stockQuote.nsmap, stockQuoteC.c, stockQuoteClient.c, stockQuoteClientLib.c, stockQuoteH.h, and stockQuoteStub.h

7. Create the Micro-service in a file. In this case, file stockQuoteMS.c is created in webservices/microservices/src/stockQuote. The structures and the call can be found at stockQuoteStub.h.

```
/*** Copyright (c) Data Intensive Cyberinfrastructure Foundation ***
*** For more information please refer to files in the COPYRIGHT directory ***/
/**
* @file      stockQuoteMS.c
*
* @brief    Access to stock quotation web services
*
* This Micro-service handles communication with http://www.webserviceX.NET
* and provides stock quotation - delayed by the web server.
*
*
* @author  Arcot Rajasekar / University of North Carolina at Chapel Hill
*/
#include "rsApiHandler.h"
#include "stockQuoteMS.h"
#include "stockQuoteH.h"
#include "stockQuote.nsmap"

int
msiGetQuote(msParam_t* inSymbolParam, msParam_t* outQuoteParam,
                ruleExecInfo_t* rei )
{
struct soap *soap = soap_new();
struct _ns1__GetQuote sym;
struct _ns1__GetQuoteResponse quote;
char response[10000];
RE_TEST_MACRO( "    Calling msiGetQuote" );
sym.symbol = (char *) inSymbolParam->inOutStruct;
soap_init(soap);
soap_set_namespaces(soap, stockQuote_namespaces);
if (soap_call___ns1__GetQuote(soap, NULL, NULL, &sym, &quote) ==
     SOAP_OK)
{
     fillMsParam( outQuoteParam, NULL, STR_MS_T, quote.GetQuoteResult,
           NULL );
     free (quote.GetQuoteResult);
```

```
        return(0);
    }
    else
    {
        sprintf(response,"Error in execution of GetQuote::%s\n",soap->buf);
        fillMsParam( outQuoteParam, NULL, STR_MS_T, response, NULL );
        return(0);
        }
    }
```

8. Create the header file for the Micro-service. In this case, file stockQuoteMS.h is created in webservices/microservice/include

```
/*** Copyright (c), Data Intensive Cyberinfrastructure Foundation
*** For more information please refer to files in the COPYRIGHT directory
***/
/**
* @file      stockQuoteMS.h
*
* @brief   Declarations for the msiStockQuote* microservices.
*/

#ifndef STOCKQUOTEMS_H /* so that it is not included multiple times by
mistake */
#define STOCKQUOTEMS_H
#include "rods.h"
#include "reGlobalsExtern.h"
#include "rsGlobalExtern.h"
#include "rcGlobalExtern.h"
int msiGetQuote( msParam_t* inSymbolParam, msParam_t* outQuoteParam,
            ruleExecInfo_t* rei );
#endif/* STOCKQUOTEMS_H */
```

9. Make sure that the header file is included in the build process. Add the following line in the file microservices.header located in webservices/microservice/include

```
#include "stockQuoteMS.h"
```

10. Add the Micro-service to the list of Micro-services that can be called by the Rule Engine. Add the following line in the file microservices.table located in webservices/microservice/include

```
{ "msiGetQuote",       2,           (funcPtr) msiGetQuote },
```

11. The next step is to change the Makefile in the webservices directory so that the new Micro-service will be compiled and linked during the build process. Add the following lines at the appropriate places in the Makefile located in the modules/webservices directory

```
        stockQuoteSrcDir= $(MSSrcDir)/stockQuote
        STOCKQUOTE_WS_OBJS = $(MSObjDir)/stockQuoteMS.o
$(MSObjDir)/stockQuoteClientLib.o
        OBJECTS +=    $(STOCKQUOTE_WS_OBJS)
        $(STOCKQUOTE_WS_OBJS): $(MSObjDir)/%.o:
$(stockQuoteSrcDir)/%.c
$(DEPEND) $(OTHER_OBJS)
        @echo "Compile webservices-stockQuote module `basename $@`. . ."
        @$(CC) –c $(CFLAGS) -o $@ $<
```

12. Compile and run: gmake clean and gmake at the iRODS top level

8.4 iRODS FUSE USER LEVEL FILE SYSTEM

FUSE (Filesystem in Userspace) is a free Unix kernel module that allows nonprivileged users to create their own file systems without editing the kernel code. This is achieved by running the file system code in user space, while the FUSE Module provides a "bridge" to the actual kernel interfaces.

The iRODS FUSE implementation allows normal users to access data stored in iRODS using standard Unix commands (ls, cp, etc.) and system calls (open, read, write, etc.).

Building iRODS FUSE:

1. Edit the config/config.mk file:

    a. Uncomment the line:

        # IRODS_FS = 1

    b. Set fuseHomeDir to the directory where the fuse library and include files are installed. For example,

fuseHomeDir=/usr/local/fuse

2. Making iRODS Fuse:

   Type in:

   cd clients/fuse
   gmake

Running iRODS Fuse:

1. cd clients/fuse/bin
2. make a local directory for mounting, for example,

   mkdir /usr/tmp/fmount

3. Set up the iRODS client env (~/irods/.irodsEnv) so that i-Commands will work. Type in:

   iinit

   and do the normal login.
4. Mount the home collection to the local directory by typing in:

   ./irodsFs/usr/tmp/fmount

5. The user's home collection is now mounted. The iRODS files and subcollections in the user's home collection should be accessible with normal Unix commands through the /usr/tmp/fmount directory.

8.5 MOUNTED iRODS COLLECTION

The -m option of the imcoll command can be used to associate (mount) an iRODS collection with a physical directory (e.g., a Unix directory) or a structured file. If the mountType is 'f' or 'filesystem', the first argument is the Unix directory path to be mounted. Only the top level collection/directory will be registered. The entire content of the registered directory can then be accessed using iRODS commands such as iput, iget, ils, and the client APIs. This is simlilar to mounting a Unix file system except that a Unix directory is mounted to an iRODS collection. For example, the following command mounts the /temp/myDir Unix directory to the /tempZone/home/myUser/mymount collection:

imcoll -m filesystem /temp/myDir /tempZone/home/myUser/mymount

An admin user will be able to mount any Unix directory. A normal user, however, needs to have a Unix account on the iRODS Server with the same name as his/her iRODS user account. Only a Unix directory created with this account can be mounted by the user. Access control to the mounted data will be based on the access permission of the mounted collection.

If the mountType is 't' or 'tar', the first argument is the iRODS logical path of a tar file that will be used as the 'structured file' for the mounted collection. The [-R resource] option is used to specify the resource to create this tar structured file in case it does not already exist. Once the tar structured file is mounted, the content of the tar file can be accessed using iRODS commands such as iput ils, iget, and the client APIs. For example, the following command mounts the iRODS tar file /tZone/home/myUser/tar/foo.tar to the /tZone/home/myUser/tarcoll collection:

```
imcoll -m tar /tZone/home/myUser/tar/foo.tar /tZone/home/myUser/tardir
```

The tar structured file implementation uses a cache on the server to cache the mounted tar file, that is, the tar file is untarred to a cache on the server before any iRODS operation. The 'ils -L' command can be used to list the properties of a mounted collection and the status of the associated cache. For example, the following is the output of the ils command:

```
C- /tZone/home/myUser/tardir  tarStructFile  /tZone/home/myUser/tar/foo.tar
/data/Vault8/rods/tar/foo.tar.cacheDir0;;;demoResc;;;1
```

The output shows that /tZone/home/myUser/tardir is a tar structured file mounted collection. The iRODS path of the tar file is in /tZone/home/myUser/tar/foo.tar. The last item actually contains three items separated by the string ;;;. It shows that the tar file is untarred into the /data/Vault8/rods/tar/foo.tar.cacheDir0 directory in the demoResc resource. The value of '1' for the last item shows that the cache content has been changed (dirty) and that the original tar file needs to be synchronized with the changes. The -s option can be used to synchronize the tar file with the cache. For example:

```
imcoll -s /tZone/home/myUser/tardir
```

The -p option can be used to purge the cache. For example,

```
imcoll -p /tZone/home/myUser/tardir
```

The -s and -p options can be used together to synchronize the tar file and then purge the cache. If the mountType is 'h' or 'haaw', the first argument is the logical path of a haaw type structured file developed by UK eScience.

NOTE: the haaw type structured file has NOT yet been implemented in iRODS.

The -U option can be used to unmount an iRODS collection. For example, the following command unmounts the /tempZone/home/myUser/mymount collection:

imcoll -U /tempZone/home/myUser/mymount

8.5.1 Building and Linking Libtar

The tar structured file implementation requires linking the iRODS Servers with the libtar library and the procedures are given below.

1. Download the Free BSD libtar software from:

   http://www.feep.net/libtar/
   http://www.freebsdsoftware.org/devel/libtar.html

2. Make the libtar software
3. Edit the config/config.mk files by uncommenting the line:

   TAR_STRUCT_FILE=1

4. Set the parameter tarDir to your libtar path; for example,
   tarDir=/data/libtar-1.2.11

5. cd to the top iRODS directory and type in "make clean; make"

It is recommended that the libtar software be installed in the same parent directory as the iRODS and PostgreSQL installation.

Also note that the current version of libtar 1.2.11 does not support tar file sizes larger than 2 Gigabytes. We have made a mod to libtar 1.2.11 so that it can handle files larger than 2 Gigabytes. This mod is only needed for building the iRODS Serversoftware. Please contact all@diceresearch.org for this mod.

8.6 iRODS DEVELOPMENT INFORMATION

iRODS is open source software and Micro-services and other features are also contributed by partners. For information on what is available and what is in the works, there is an "iRODS Development Information" page with these details in the wiki at https://www.irods.org. This section contains iRODS Release Notes with descriptions of features, bug fixes, and other information for each iRODS release; Extensions, with current and in development features, interfaces, drivers, and additional functionalities for iRODS, including contributed software; a Wish List with user requests for features and extensions to iRODS; an iRODS Roadmap of iRODS future development path; and a Contributor's page on contributing code to iRODS, with the Contributor's Agreement.

• • • •

APPENDIX A
iRODS Shell Commands

The i-Commands available in release 2.2 of iRODS are listed below, organized by type. The few parameters the i-Commands need to operate (for connection to an iRODS Server) can be set as user Environment Variables, or specified on the command line. There is a common set of command line options for the i-Commands, so that each option (-a, -b, -c, etc.) will mean the same thing (generally) in all of them. 'iinit' writes an automatic login file (with scrambled password) for you in any window on your computer (actually, any computer with your same home directory); otherwise, i-Commands will prompt for your password.

You can display a current list of i-Commands by typing

ihelp

The options available for a specific i-Command can be found by using the help option "-h". For example:

iinit –h

Creates a file containing your iRODS password in a scrambled form, to be used automatically by the i-Commands.

Usage: iinit [-ehvVl]

- e echo the password as you enter it (normally there is no echo)
- l list the iRODS Environment Variables (only)
- v verbose
- V Very verbose
- h this help

A.1 ENVIRONMENT VARIABLES (EXAMPLE VALUES ARE SHOWN FOR EACH VARIABLE)

irodsHost=localhost	The IP address of the iCAT metadata catalog server.
irodsPort=1247	The port number used by the iCAT metadata catalog.

irodsDefResource=MzResc	The logical name of the default storage resource.
irodsHome=/Mzone/home/Mzrods	The user home collection within the Data Grid.
irodsCwd=/Mzone/home/Mzrods	The current working collection within the Data Grid.
irodsUserName=Mzrods	The user name known by the Data Grid.
irodsZone=Mzone	The name of the Data Grid.

A.2 USER AND FILE MANIPULATION I-COMMANDS

iinit	Initialize—Store your password in a scrambled form for automatic use by other i-Commands
iput	Store a file
iget	Get a file
imkdir	Like mkdir, make an iRODS collection (similar to a directory or Windows folder)
ichmod	Like chmod, allow (or later restrict) access to your data objects by other users
icp	Like cp or rcp, copy an iRODS data object
irm	Like rm, remove an iRODS data object
ils	Like ls, list iRODS data objects (files) and collections (directories)
ipwd	Like pwd, print the iRODS current working directory
icd	Like cd, change the iRODS current working directory
irepl	Replicate data objects
iexit	Logout (use 'iexit full' to remove your scrambled password from the disk)
ipasswd	Change your iRODS password
ichksum	Checksum one or more data-objects or collections from iRODS space
imv	Moves/renames an iRODS data-object or collection
iphymv	Physically move files in iRODS to another storage resource
ireg	Register a file or a directory of files and subdirectory into iRODS
irmtrash	Remove one or more data-objects or collections from an iRODS trash bin

irsync	Synchronize the data between a local copy and the copy stored in iRODS or between two iRODS copies
itrim	Trims down the number of replicas of a file in iRODS by deleting some replicas
iexecmd	Remotely Execute (fork and exec) a command on the server
imcoll	Manage (mount, unmount, synchronize, and purge of a cache) a mounted iRODS collection and the associated cache
ibun	Upload and download structured (e.g., tar) files

A.3 METADATA I-COMMANDS

imeta	Add, remove, list, or query user-defined Attribute–Value–Unit triplets metadata
isysmeta	Show or modify system metadata
iquest	Query (pose a question to) the iCAT via an SQL-like interface

A.4 INFORMATIONAL i-COMMANDS

ienv	Show current iRODS environment
ilsresc	List resources
iuserinfo	List users
imiscsvrinfo	Get basic server information; test communication
ierror	Convert an iRODS error code to text
ihelp	Display a list of the i-Commands

A.5 ADMINISTRATION i-COMMANDS

iadmin	Administration commands: add/remove/modify users, resources, etc.
iphysbun	Physically bundle files for efficient storage to tape

A.6 RULES AND DELAYED RULE EXECUTION i-COMMANDS

irule	Submit a user defined Rule to be executed by an iRODS Server

iqstat	Show pending iRODS Rule executions
iqdel	Removes delayed Rules from the queue
iqmod	Modifies delayed Rules in the queue

As an example of the i-Commands, we list the help package for the iquest command. For each i-Command, invoking the –h parameter will display the input parameters and provide usage examples.

Usage: iquest [[hint] format] selectConditionString

format is C format restricted to character strings.

selectConditionString is of the form:

SELECT <attribute> [, <attribute>]* [WHERE <condition> [AND <condition>]*]

attribute can be found using iquest attrs command

condition is of the form: <attribute><rel-op><value>

rel-op is a relational operator: e.g., =, <>, >,<, like, not like, between, etc.,

value is either a constant or a wild-carded expression.

One can also use a few aggregation operators such as sum, count, min, max, and avg. Use % and _ as wild-cards, and use \ to escape them.

Options are:

-h this help

Examples:

iquest "SELECT DATA_NAME, DATA_CHECKSUM WHERE DATA_RESC_NAME like 'demo%'"

iquest "For %-12.12s size is %s" "SELECT DATA_NAME, DATA_SIZE WHERE COLL_NAME = '/tempZone/home/rods'"

iquest "SELECT COLL_NAME WHERE COLL_NAME like '/tempZone/home/%'"

iquest "User %-6.6s has %-5.5s access to file %s" "SELECT USER_NAME, DATA_ACCESS_NAME, DATA_NAME WHERE COLL_NAME = '/tempZone/home/rods'" iquest " %-5.5s access has been given to user %-6.6s for the file %s" "SELECT DATA_ACCESS_NAME, USER_NAME, DATA_NAME WHERE COLL_NAME = '/tempZone/home/rods'"

iquest "SELECT RESC_NAME, RESC_LOC, RESC_VAULT_PATH, DATA_PATH WHERE DATA_NAME = 't2' AND COLL_NAME = '/tempZone/home/rods'"

iquest "User %-9.9s users %-14.14s bytes in %8.8s files in %s" "SELECT USER_NAME, sum(DATA_SIZE),count(DATA_NAME),RESC_NAME"

iquest "select sum(DATA_SIZE) where COLL_NAME = '/tempZone/home/rods'"

iquest "select sum(DATA_SIZE) where COLL_NAME like '/tempZone/home/rods%'"

iquest "select sum(DATA_SIZE), RESC_NAME where COLL_NAME like '/tempZone/home/rods%'"

APPENDIX B

Rulegen Grammar

B.1 GRAMMAR OF THE RULEGEN LANGUAGE

The reserved words used by the rulegen program are listed below:

```
program
        : program rule_list inputs outputs
        ;
inputs
        : INPUT inp_expr_list
        ;
outputs
        : OUTPUT out_expr_list
        ;
rule_list
        : rule
        | rule rule_list
        ;
rule
        : action_def '{' first_statement '}'
        | action_def '{' first_statement statement_list '}'
        ;
action_def
        : action_name
        | action_name '(' arg_list ')'
        ;
microserve
        : action_name
        | action_name '(' arg_list ')'
        ;
```

```
action_name
        : identifier
        ;
arg_list
        : arg_val
        | arg_val ',' arg_list
        ;
arg_val
        : STR_LIT
        | Q_STR_LIT
        | NUM_LIT
        ;
first_statement
        :  selection_statement
        |
        ;
compound_statement
        : '{' '}'
        | '{' statement_list '}'
        ;
statement_list
        : statement
        | statement_list statement
        ;
statement
        : selection_statement
        | iteration_statement
        | compound_statement
        | action_statement ';'
        | ass_expr ';'
        | execution_statement
        ;
selection_statement
        : ON '(' cond_expr ')' statement
        | ON '(' cond_expr ')' statement or_list_statement_list
        ;
```

```
iteration_statement
        : WHILE '(' cond_expr ')' statement
        | FOR '(' ass_expr_list ';' cond_expr ';' ass_expr_list ')' statement
        | IF '(' cond_expr ')' THEN statement
        | IF '(' cond_expr ')' THEN statement ELSE statement
        | 'break'
        ;
or_list_statement_list
        : ORON '(' cond_expr ')' statement
        | OR statement
        | ORON '(' cond_expr ')' statement or_list_statement_list
        | OR statement or_list_statement_list
        ;
action_statement
        : microserve ACRAC_SEP microserve
        | microserve
        ;
execution_statement
        : DELAY '(' cond_expr ')' statement
        | REMOTE '(' identifier ',' cond_expr ')' statement
        | PARALLEL '(' cond_expr ')' statement
        | ONEOF statement
        | SOMEOF '(' identifier ')' statement
        | FOREACH '(' identifier ')' statement
        ;
```

B.2 EXPRESSIONS USED BY THE RULEGEN PARSER

```
inp_expr
    : identifier '=' cond_expr
    ;
inp_expr_list
    : inp_expr
    | inp_expr ',' inp_expr_list
    ;
out_expr
```

```
        : arg_val
out_expr_list
        : out_expr
        | out_expr ',' out_expr_list
        ;
ass_expr
        : identifier  '=' cond_expr
ass_expr_list
        : ass_expr
        | ass_expr ',' ass_expr_list
        ;
cond_expr
        : logical_expr
        | '(' logical_expr ')'
        | cond_expr AND_OP cond_expr
        | cond_expr OR_OP cond_expr
        | cond_expr '+'  cond_expr
        | cond_expr '-'  cond_expr
        ;
logical_expr
        : TRUE
        | FALSE
        | relational_expr
        | logical_expr EQ_OP logical_expr
        | logical_expr NE_OP logical_expr
        | logical_expr '<' logical_expr
        | logical_expr '>' logical_expr
        | logical_expr LE_OP logical_expr
        | logical_expr GE_OP logical_expr
        | logical_expr LIKE logical_expr
        | logical_expr NOT LIKE logical_expr
        ;
relational_expr
        :  STR_LIT
        |  NUM_LIT
        |  Q_STR_LIT
```

```
      ;
identifier
      : STR_LIT
      | Q_STR_LIT
      | NUM_LIT
      ;

STR_LIT    : string of characters
Q_STR_LIT  : quoted (") string of characters
NUM_LIT    : number-string
AND_OP     : "&&"
OR_OP      :"||"
LE_O       :"<="
GE_OP      :">="
EQ_OP      :"=="
NE_OP      :"!="
ACRAC_SE   :":::"
```

APPENDIX C

Exercises

A student that takes a class on policy-based data management should be able to answer the following questions about the iRODS Data Grid. They are divided into short factual questions and longer essay-style questions:

C.1 SHORT QUESTIONS

- Explain what **core.irb** is and what role it plays within an implementation of iRODS.
- Explain what the **iCAT** is and what role it plays within an implementation of iRODS.
- For a given Rule, identify **two** different ways that you could invoke the Rule (i.e., make the Rule run within iRODS). For each of these two ways to invoke the Rule, provide one reason why you might decide to choose it over the other way.
- Identify the software that needs to be installed on your computer in order to run an iRODS client.
- Identify the software that needs to be installed on your computer in order to run a complete iRODS Data Grid.
- Briefly explain the relationship between: (1) a policy and a Rule, and (2) a Rule and Micro-service.
- List the **four** main parts of an iRODS Rule. Provide an example an actual iRODS Rule that includes all four of these parts.
- Identify and briefly explain **three** different types of events that can trigger an iRODS Rule.
- Provide a human language explanation of a **condition** that you could specify in a Rule.
- Provide a human language explanation of a **recovery set** that you could specify in a Rule.
- Identify **three** different ways in which interactions between independent data grids can be **federated**.
- Identify **two** different iRODS clients and briefly explain **one** potential advantage and **one** potential disadvantage of using each as a way to access an iRODS Data Grid.
- Identify **two** i-Commands and briefly explain what each one does.

- Identify **two** system Micro-services and briefly explain what each one does.
- Explain what a whiteboard variable is and provide **two** examples.
- Explain the purpose of the delayExec Micro-service and provide **one** example (either using iRule syntax or explained in human language) of how delayExec could be used.
- Explain the purpose of the forEachExec Micro-service and provide **one** example (either using iRule syntax or explained in human language) of how forEachExec could be used.
- Explain the purpose of the writeLine Micro-service and provide one example (either using iRule syntax or explained in human language) of how writeLine could be used.
- Explain what "nop" means when it is included in an iRODS Rule.
- Identify **one** command and **two** Micro-services that can be used to query iCAT. Briefly explain the main differences between these three approaches.
- Provide **two** examples (either using iRule syntax or explained in human language) of actions that a repository might want to carry out each time the acCreateUser Micro-service is executed.
- Identify the **three** main parts of an iRule inputFile and provide **one** example for each part.
- Explain what a Persistent State Variable is and provide **two** examples.
- Explain why there are two different syntaxes for writing Rules in iRODS and identify a way to translate from the more human-readable to the more compact version.
- Explain **two** different ways to change the core.irb file.
- Explain **one** way in which the iRule language is particularly sensitive to small differences in what you type into the Rule and provide **one** example (either using iRule syntax or explained in human language) of how this sensitivity could cause you trouble when trying execute a Rule.

C.2 ESSAY QUESTIONS

- Explain what a data grid is and the key capabilities of the iRODS Data Grid system. Explain how a scientific research project might use an iRODS Data Grid. Explain how a library might use an iRODS Data Grid. Explain how an archive might use an iRODS Data Grid.
- Draw a diagram of an iRODS Data Grid and explain the architecture.
- Explain the main challenges of sharing distributed data and how iRODS approaches this.
- Explain the main challenges of managing large-scale distributed digital data and how iRODS approaches this.
- Explain the main challenges of preserving digital data and how iRODS approaches this.

- Identify and explain something about iRODS that could be **improved**. Be specific about (1) what the problem is, (2) why you see it as a problem, and (3) how it could be fixed (not a detailed proposal for how to implement the fix, but just an explanation of what could be done to fix it).
- Identify and explain what you see as the **three** most important **challenges** to an institution that would like to implement iRODS. Be specific about (1) what the challenges are and (2) why you think they are important.
- Your institution has installed DSpace and is using it to manage various digital collections. Your boss has been told that she should also consider implementing iRODS. She is a very thoughtful and responsible administrator but is not familiar with iRODS, data grids, or the mechanics of programming. She has asked you to explain to her why iRODS would be worth considering, given that DSpace is already up and running successfully. Provide **two** reasons why she might want to consider iRODS. For each reason, provide an explanation and an example to illustrate your point. (Note: You should assume that your institution is successfully applying the existing features of DSpace, so your answer should focus on core capabilities of the software, rather than the usability of DSpace.)
- Identify one of the criteria from the Trustworthy Repositories Audit & Certification: Criteria and Checklist (TRAC). Provide human language (i.e., not in iRODS syntax) description of (1) a Rule that could be used to meet that criterion and (2) how you could determine whether the Rule had done what you intended it to do.
- iRODS is designed to support "data virtualization." Explain what this means and why it is desirable. In your answer, provide **three** examples of data virtualization within iRODS.
- iRODS is designed to support "policy virtualization." Explain what this means and why it is desirable in general. Then use **one** specific example of a policy being "virtualized" in iRODS and **two** specific reasons why policy virtualization would be beneficial in this case.
- Identify and explain **three** characteristics of a policy that increase the chances that someone will be able to write iRODS Rules to enforce the policy.
- Explain the differences between atomic, deferred, and periodic Rules. Provide **one** example (either using iRule syntax or explained in human language) of each.

Describe **two** different cases in which delayed execution of a Rule (or set of Rules) would be desirable, and describe **two** different cases in which delayed execution of a Rule (or set of Rules) would be undesirable.

Author Biographies

Arcot Rajasekar is a professor in the School of Library and Information Sciences at the University of North Carolina, Chapel Hill, and a chief scientist at the Renaissance Computing Institute (RENCI). Previously, he was at the San Diego Supercomputer Center at the University of California, San Diego, leading the Data Grids Technology Group. He has been involved in research and development of data grid middleware systems for over a decade and is a lead originator behind the concepts in the Storage Resource Broker (SRB) and the integrated Rule Oriented Data Systems (iRODS), two premier data grid middleware developed by the Data Intensive Cyber Environments Group. Dr. Rajasekar has a Ph.D. in computer science from the University of Maryland at College Park and has more than 100 publications in the areas of data grids, logic programming, deductive databases, digital library, and persistent archives.

Reagan Moore is a professor in the School of Information and Library Science at the University of North Carolina, Chapel Hill, chief scientist for Data Intensive Cyber Environments at the Renaissance Computing Institute, and director of the Data Intensive Cyber Environments Center at University of North Carolina. He coordinates research efforts in development of data grids, digital libraries, and preservation environments. Developed software systems include the Storage Resource Broker data grid and the integrated Rule-Oriented Data System. Supported projects include the National Archives and Records Administration Transcontinental Persistent Archive Prototype, and science data grids for seismology, oceanography, climate, high-energy physics, astronomy, and bioinformatics. An ongoing research interest is use of data grid technology to automate execution of management policies and validate trustworthiness of repositories. Dr. Moore's previous roles include the following: director of the DICE group at the San Diego Supercomputer Center, and Manager of production services at SDSC. He previously worked as a computational plasma physicist at General Atomics on equilibrium and stability of toroidal fusion devices. He has a Ph.D. in plasma physics from the University of California, San Diego (1978), and a B.S. in physics from the California Institute of Technology (1967).

Chien-Yi Hou is a research associate at School of Information and Library Science (SILS) in University of North Carolina, Chapel Hill. He is also a member of the Sustainable Archives &

Library Technologies (SALT) Laboratory and a member of the Data Intensive Cyber Environments (DICE) group. Chien-Yi Hou's interests include data grid, digital archiving, information management, and databases. Before joining SILS, he worked at the San Diego Supercomputer Center (SDSC) as Digital Preservation Specialist. He has a master's degree in computer science from the University of California, San Diego (UCSD), and he received his bachelor's degree in computer and information science from the National Chiao Tung University, Taiwan.

Christopher A. Lee is assistant professor at the School of Information and Library Science at the University of North Carolina, Chapel Hill. He teaches classes in archival administration, records management, digital curation, understanding information technology for managing digital collections, and the construction of digital repository rules. His research focuses on long-term curation of digital collections and stewardship (by individuals and information professionals) of personal digital archives.

Richard Marciano is a professor in the School of Information and Library Science at University of North Carolina, Chapel Hill, and chief scientist for Persistent Archives and Digital Preservation at the Renaissance Computing Institute (RENCI). He is director of the Sustainable Archives & Library Technologies (SALT) Laboratory and a member of the Data Intensive Cyber Environments (DICE) Group. Dr. Marciano has conducted research and development in preservation environments for the last decade on projects funded by NARA, NSF, NHPRC, LOC and IMLS. Richard Marciano holds a postdoctoral degree in computational geography, a Ph.D. in computer science from the University of Iowa, and a B.S. in electrical engineering and avionics.

Antoine de Torcy has been with the DICE group since 2003, at the University of California, San Diego, until 2008, and now at the University of North Carolina, Chapel Hill. Antoine has been involved in the development of Data Grid software, first with the Storage Resource Broker (SRB) and its successor, the Rule Oriented Data System (iRODS), implementing client interfaces for SRB and server modules for iRODS. He has been working on the Electronic Records Archive (ERA) project, using and extending iRODS to meet the list of ERA requirements, and building prototypes. His technical expertise has helped various groups build preservation environments based on iRODS and focused on data and metadata. Antoine holds an engineering degree in applied mathematics and computer science from the University of Paris–Dauphine.

Michael Wan leads the DICE (Data Intensive Cyber Environment) group of INC (Institute of Neural Science) at University of California, San Diego. He is the chief software architect of the

Integrated Rule-Oriented Data System (iRODS) and the Storage Resource Broker (SRB). iRODS is a follow-on of SRB. It is a state-of-the-art production quality data grid software. The software supports data sharing, data publication, and data preservation. It is a rule-based system that can be used to automate the enforcement of data management policies and validation of assessment criteria. Before SRB, Michael has spent 10 years developing operating systems and archival storage systems at SDSC. Michael received his B.S. degree from Illinois State University and M.S. from Georgia Institute of Technology.

Wayne Schroeder is a senior software engineer with the iRODS team and, with Dr. Arcot Rajasekar and Michael Wan, designed and developed the core iRODS system. His contributions include the database catalog interface, administration tools, metadata interfaces, security/authentication, and installation and testing subsystems. He has over 30 years of experience in software engineering, with expertise in data management, computer security, networking, scientific applications, high-performance computing, and system support/administration. He earned a B.S. in computer science in 1976, magna cum laude, with a minor in psychology.

Sheau-Yen Chen is Data Intensive Cyber Environment (DICE) Center's Data Grid System Administrator for iRODS. Before DICE, she was with San Diego Supercomputer Center (SDSC) as a programmer/analyst and administered the Storage Resource Broker (SRB). She gained valuable experience as SRB system administrator since 2001. Before moving to California, she worked with Solucient (company that produced 100 top hospitals), University of Michigan's Department of Radiology, Motoresearch, Northern Telecom, and Dictaphone R&D Center as computer programmer/analyst. Sheau-Yen has an M.S. degree in biostatistics from Virginia Commonwealth University and another M.S. degree in Mathematics from Virginia State University.

Paul Tooby is the community development coordinator of the Data Intensive Cyberinfrastructure Foundation, home of the growing iRODS open source community. In addition to extensive experience in scientific communication, he has a B.A. in physics from Swarthmore College and graduate work in Oceanography at the Scripps Institution of Oceanography.

Bing Zhu is a computational scientist in the Data Intensive Cyber Environment Center. Dr. Bing received a Ph.D. degree in the joint computational science program by Claremont Graduate University and San Diego State University. His research interests include digital archive and preservation, distributed data management, high-performance computing, and computational fluid dynamics.